Lucy Swimming
and other poems

Fiona Kaplan

Grosvenor House
Publishing Limited

The right of Fiona Kaplan to be identified as the author of this
work has been asserted in accordance with Section 78
of the Copyright, Designs and Patents Act 1988

This book is published by
Grosvenor House Publishing Ltd
Link House
140 The Broadway, Tolworth, Surrey, KT6 7HT.
www.grosvenorhousepublishing.co.uk

A CIP record for this book
is available from the British Library

ISBN 978-1-83975-110-3

For Paul, Lucy and Chloe

All proceeds from the sale of this book will be donated to the Coventry Resource Centre for the Blind, a registered charity which provides practical and social support for blind and partially-sighted people, their families and carers.

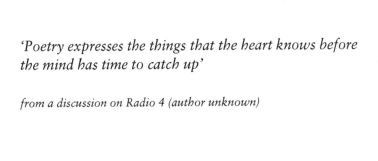

'Poetry expresses the things that the heart knows before the mind has time to catch up'

from a discussion on Radio 4 (author unknown)

This book is semi-fictional; it is not intended as a factually accurate account of my experiences. Some names and places and other identifying details have been changed in order to protect the privacy of the individuals concerned.

Contents

Part 1
Child

okāsan no aji

The taste of the mother

I am allowed to crack the eggs and
Try to separate the whites from the yolks
My mother quick but patient
Laughs at the spills
Hesitant at first
I begin to enjoy the sharp precise crack
Crack! of the curved shell split in two at the equator
Juggling the outpouring yolk between the fragile cups
Sharp-edged
Fingers nimble and quick
I must not burst the filmy skin holding the soft yellow
    ball
Ropes of thick clear viscous 'white' are dripping into
    the glass bowl
Fascinating and slightly repulsive
My mother doesn't like cream
So it's all about the meringue
Her light swift confident hand
Whisks the unpromising greyish puddle with the funny
    old steel utensil
Frothing foaming
Until improbably white peaks stand up in the glacier of
    the bowl
Sugar vanilla vinegar
We form a round crater with the glossy lava and
Watch it solidify through the window of the oven

3

Later we slide out
The delicate softly-scented vanilla structure
(Don't touch!)
A Gaudi-esque edifice
From the garden I have fetched
A warm just-ripened peach
We slice fragrant fine yellow-orange crescents and I
Make an inlay of spiral mosaic in the soft cream
Here and there I see fissures and erosion
Cracks in the futuristic balustrade
But my mother laughs again
And deftly daubs them with blobs of cream
Beautiful and so ephemeral
Crumbling white elfin Midsummer Night's Dream castle
Surprise of crisp shell and
Soft interior
Sugar and sharp fruit on my tongue
Consummate skill
Delicate and elegant
Pavlova was a singer I say, absent-mindedly
And am corrected politely by my friend
She was a ballet dancer
Of course.

Crimes and Misdemeanours or
The Right to Roam

I am dangling by my ankles over the bannisters of the first floor landing, the carpeted floor so unbelievably far below that I close my eyes and cannot look. Maybe five or six years old, I line up and accept the dizzy horror of this punishment, along with my brother (four or five) and his friend. We realise we have gone too far this time. Andrew is very cross. I cannot remember the transgression. It may have been the time we decided to clean his bike for him, taking the beautiful racer apart and carefully cleaning and oiling all the fascinating shiny cogs and levers; it was soon uncomfortably apparent to us that we had no idea how to put it all back together again. Andrew is a very big boy (about twelve) and, as elder brother of our friend, has been told to keep an eye on us while we play at their house. I like him, as he complimented me on my Lego construction skills, much to the boys' chagrin.

Punishment meted out, we were soon happily back to our usual pursuits. We had an old children's record player with some orange 78s, including *The Lambton Worm* (which was actually a dragon) and *The Camptown Races*, perhaps from my mother's family in the North East? and then we discovered Andrew's stash of black shiny new Beatles 45s. 'Can't buy me love!' we carolled joyously … 'We all live in a yellow submarine'. Maybe we had overstepped the mark or damaged one of these. Or teaching ourselves to play billiards on the lovely old half-size table in the garage, we occasionally made a small furrow through the tempting green baize as we pursued the heavy brightly coloured balls with the long unwieldy adult cues, pointy ends carefully primed with blue chalk by our small fingers. And occasionally, the precise fat *toc!* when we hit the ball fairly and squarely in the centre and the intense satisfaction of potting it *plop!* into the little string net … I doubt we were supposed to do that either.

We pored over the book of boobs we found in Andrew's cupboard and locked ourselves in the downstairs loo together to compare our four-year-old body parts (unfair, I thought, as I was the only girl). Of course, we had no idea what they were for, though my brother, noting his two 'baked beans', deduced that there was one to make each child (we were a two-child family). A permanent Scalextric track snaked in and out of Andrew's bedroom. I never tired of revving the glamourous F1 cars down the long black straights, easing the throttle around the bend and then flying off the track on the treacherous chicane, into the pit stops for a quick repair. The only thing that beat that was driving the bumper cars at the fair and the mysteriously dark and good-looking traveller boy stepping like a dancer from car to car for the money and telling me I would be the next Pat Moss.

A little older (maybe eight or nine) long summer days were spent out 'on our bikes' going fishing at Eathorpe with bamboo poles and wire hooks tied on with string. 'Look!', says my brother, 'an aeroplane' (we were just passing Baginton). I look up and it is a lovely tiny private plane and then I am in the ditch in a bed of nettles, fortunately unhurt. The boys are chortling at my absent-minded steering error.

Efficiently we mend the punctures in our inner tubes with a washing up bowl of water, inflating the tired old much-repaired rubber tubes with our bike pumps. Locating the leak by the tiny stream of silver bubbles rising up to the surface, we dry the rubber around the hole, grating some of the smooth grey chalk and dusting it on, then carefully applying the clear runny adhesive with the interesting smell and waiting until it is sticky before smoothing on the patch. I like how neatly everything fits back into the oval blue repair kit tin. I snap it shut and zip it in my saddle bag.

I am allowed to run down the road for a few minutes to see if there are any little frogs yet in the pond and, fascinated by the wriggling tadpoles, leeches and dragonfly larvae and the water boatmen impossibly skittering across the skin of the water, I overbalance into the green slimy waters in my best black party dress and white lace tights. I am not alarmed by the shallow waters of the pond, but the prospect of explaining this to my mother is truly daunting.

Like all children, we form a club, which meets on the ridge of the shed roof, our vantage point; in our pockets a matchbox with a tiny brass cartridge top (for a whistle), a match (we never lit anything), a tiny pencil, paper and piece of string. Our codes are written in invisible ink and when a new boy we don't like gets annoying I ask him how many noughts there are in two hundred. I have no idea but neither has he, so he cries and runs away. Trainers do not yet exist. My father threatens to put steel toecaps on my good leather school lace-ups if I scuff them any more climbing those walls and trees (it is the skinhead era).

Andrew suspends me by the armpits: he's a whirling dervish now and I'm a circus acrobat, flying out horizontally, galvanised by terror and exhilaration in equal parts. My brother's turn and I get too close, his sandal buckle hits my knee, there is quite a deep hole and I can see it is not red in there but a funny purply-black. I do not cry (we don't) but I know it is bad. We don't tell our parents and it heals. I look down now on my right leg and see the little pale shiny scar, still there.

One day some tiny little shrivelled frogs black from the sun are lying in the hot stone desert of the edging of the pond. I see how fragile life is.

Freewheeling down the hill no hands I am entranced by a gorgeous golden yellow E-type, icon of the Jaguars made in my city and I crash into a humbler vehicle parked opposite. Out flies the owner, apoplectic, yelling at me for the long deep groove I have scored in the bodywork, but my father shouts back that it is the child that matters, not the car. By this time he has taken out a family third party insurance policy.

In the garden is our first car, a bright red pedal vehicle found in the small ads in the Evening Telegraph. It cracks, we cry, but it is given a new lease of life by colleagues of my father in the welding workshop at the

Technical College. He teaches chemistry there. He sits me on the huge mahogany laboratory benches beside the tall glass cases of experimental apparatus and I drop copper salts into the beaker of water glass, fascinated by this new sort of pond. My father thought to make a scientist of me, but all I really wanted was to look at the tall slim stalagmites of bright blue copper crystals that grew up so beautiful and perfect in this strange sterile underwater world.

Sunburnt and dark-eyed nomad, only just returned from a whole month under canvas in the South of France, my parents teachers with long holidays to wander where we willed, with my short brown bob and preference for shorts, my mother saw I did not settle well amongst the Disneyland princesses of my infant school. And so it was I found myself instead at Mrs Leeding's nature table, discussing names of shells and insects. No doubt it was a sort of interview. I must have passed because I got the job, in my clear handwriting with dipper pen and ink, of labelling the shell collection, consulting the *Observer Book of Nature* with my friend.

What joy! a place so right for me that only momentary clouds (the four times table and the sewing class) would float briefly across my six-year-old sky. I often forgot to bring my sewing bag to school. Instead, quietly and patiently I worked with my friend, poking bits of thread and pins through a knothole in the wooden classroom floor to help the *Borrowers*. After all, they just might need them.

I am a tomboy in my shorts and shirt, my gang of three; in vain my mother dreams of buying little frocks for me, but sensibly resigns herself and takes me down to London where we see the premiere of *The Sound of Music* ; I remember it to this day.

And then when I am ten Fiona moves in up the road and I am sent to see 'if she would like to play?' She is my age, and new to Coventry. I finally acknowledge I'm a girl, whatever that may mean.

Fire

Saturday afternoon a bit bored I go off to the garden
    centre
Just before closing time
To buy a larger plant pot for my ailing camellia
The pots are too big but on the way in
Something catches my eye
I do not need it
I am not going to buy it
But I can't help looking at it
Going back and looking again
Measuring how tall it would be
Looking again at the photo on the box
It is so elegant
Simple and shapely
I could probably build it myself
Flushed with confidence and pride (or is it hubris ?)
After my success with my new Ikea chairs
Reader, I bought it
I get out the small blue slightly rusty toolbox
My father gave me when his fingers got too stiff
With adjustable spanner crosshead screwdriver pliers
Remembering all the things we two built together
I set out all the pieces hearing my father's maxims
Check everything is there before you do anything
I study the diagram for once very clear and laugh
If all else fails follow the instructions
Start to make the graceful black wrought-iron basket

From three springy curved sections smelling pleasantly
    like engine oil
Add the legs and base and now I can stand it upright
Don't screw the bolts too tight until it's all together
It is enjoyable needs full concentration
Whiles away an hour or so cat watching warily
You won't like this I say teasingly
Greasy black nuts and bolts take me back again
We are assembling the children's climbing frame
One or two bolts a few millimetres out but it held up
    for years
Everything in place now with my pliers I tighten each
    fixing
It is just as gorgeous as the photo on the box
Garden's a bit small just not too sure if it will set the
    fence on fire
Childhood delight of autumn and Guy Fawkes Night
Flames shooting house-high from the rather large
    bonfire
Father laughing mother fretting
Roasting potatoes foil-wrapped in the embers
Christmas Eve after mass in beautiful Majorcan
    mountain church
Standing round brazier warming hands with villagers
Fire food and laughter under a deep midwinter sky

'Mummy Attenborough'

My daughter plays the clip to herself on her phone and
    laughs
Show me! I say
I see butterflies poised on pebbles in the ravine
Semi-shade of branches overhanging dry stream bed
The end of the beach
I hear my voice unaware relaxed and happy
Amazing ! all these colours and patterns ... all in one
    place!
Right by the sea! Have they really all just emerged
    today?
Look at that lime one! Is that a red admiral?
They are so much bigger here in Greece!
And maybe that's a swallowtail, really extraordinary!
We used to see them all the time
As a child I sat so still they
Settled on the flowers on my dress
Now here so unexpectedly
Drawn to our bright beach clothes unafraid
Unbelievably fragile long black legs alight on us
Full of grace
For one propitious moment
Out of time

The House Where I Grew Up

I have almost driven past the road when I decide to take the turn and visit the house I where I grew up. I realise it is actually quite a big house, a 1930s semi. Approaching with some nostalgia and not a little trepidation, I am reassured. Our solid and comfortable family home has been gently modernised with much care and attention to detail.

The magnolia tree, planted by my South Shields grandmother in her delight at being able to grow blossoming trees in Warwickshire after the harsh winters of the North East, has grown into a beautiful dome of large deep green pendant leaves, sprinkled now with yellow and brown and screening the double bay windows.

The cherry tree and almond planted for me and my brother grew so big that they had to be removed eventually, but bright pink and purple graceful nodding lanterns of fuschia and the black berries of the little shrub I didn't like are still visible over the low brick wall of the front garden, beside the gentle curve of the dark blue block paved drive around the lawn put in by my mother. A small shiny red car is parked neatly on it now. I remember grass and concrete paving slabs, my father's neat and functional DIY, and our 1960s orange VW camper van.

Now the windows have modern double glazing with carefully-chosen rectangular panes in the style of the house. I am childishly delighted to see that the owners have retained the distinctive oak front door with its small eye level central coloured glazed panel and spy hole, sensibly adding an enclosed glass porch. The scruffy old wooden up and over door leading to the double garage has given way to a new brick facade and through the blinds I glimpse a young man working at a spacious desk in a new sunlit home office.

Above the door an exact copy of the distinctive and probably unique stained-glass landing window greets me with its lovely sunrise, much loved by me as a child and yet quite forgotten until this moment.

I cannot see the big garden behind the house and I am glad. It has almost certainly been carefully landscaped and put in order. I prefer to remember the slightly chaotic place of my childhood, a surprisingly large space, rectangular and long enough for us to pack our sandwiches when we were very small and play 'going to Birmingham' down at the bottom of the garden by the rickety shed. It was mostly a rough lawn for us to play on, with four tall old cooking apple trees where we hung our rope hammocks and stayed out in our sleeping bags all night; we crossed from tree to tree like monkeys high above the ground and fetched down the best apples for my mother's pies.

My girls, not tomboys, so much more sedate, made us a restaurant with small flowers to mark our places, on the huge patio my father laid himself in the sixties, where in summer we could all eat outside at the broad grey teak table.

Those were good days, I see now, fractious and impatient as we of course sometimes were. This house has seen four generations of my family. I notice it is time to go. I start my car and drive away.

I will not interrogate my memories too far, or like the filmy multi-coloured bubbles caught by children they may burst and disappear.

Part 2

Greece

Efnisi

Out in the bay
Beach people bright tiny muted by distance
Late in day stillness
We swim together
Synchronised
Sea level
Playing like dolphins

Swallows are swooping
Scooping up insects in confident
Arcs across the sea
Skimming the surface
Eye level
So close
Last minute
Powerful body climbs upward
Tattoo of throat markings rust and deep blue
Strong slender flexed curved wings
Delicate tail fins spread wide and lift up
Effortless into the afternoon sun

On the horizon
Lazy blue mountains
Hazy soft female reclining half-watching
Somnolent sentient
Mythical indolent gift of the gods
Indifferent
Ithaca sleeps

Homage to Kefalonia

Zoe caught sight of the boat in the harbour and felt a rush of excitement spiced with not a little trepidation. What had she been thinking, signing up for a marine adventure ? It was all very well for her daughter, half her age, but how would she ever manage to cope with that mask and tube. Some unpleasant memories flooded back ... she could almost feel those ill-fitting goggles pushing uncomfortably into her face, the smell of old rubber, then the glass slowly steaming up and filling with water until she couldn't see a thing. She put this disagreeable, slightly panicky feeling out of her head and focused on the rather attractive young Italian who was explaining how he had refurbished his lovely wooden boat. It was an old cargo boat dating from 1946. It had criss-crossed these channels between the islands, Kefalonia to Ithaca, Lefkada, Meganisi, captained by just one man alone, delivering coal. Today we would have two crew, the blond and curly-headed angelic Fabio and his very competent-looking dark-haired Kefalonian mate Vassily, coiling the mooring rope expertly out of the way on the deck.

'The boat is sinking. I have disappeared overboard and Vassily ... is dead!' pronounced Fabio dramatically with a huge grin. There was an shocked murmur from the assembled Brits, clearly a very pleasant gathering of old friends holidaying together and mostly in their late sixties. 'What will you do?' He had everyone's attention. He produced a life-jacket with a flourish and randomly selected a slight and petite suntanned woman who valiantly rose to the occasion. Fabio stood and enjoyed the performance, as with much hilarity she was instructed by various members of the group, happily contradicting each other in good-humoured fashion, until the jacket was on and whistle at the ready to summon help. That is a good teacher, thought Zoe, her professional training assessing the man and his methods, and all at once she felt everything would be fine, they were in safe hands.

The old boat chugged comfortably across the channel and Zoe and her daughter chatted to the others. As it happened, they were a well-travelled group, with quite a few language teachers and enjoyed the opportunity to find out all about Sarah's studies in Italian and French, her job, life in Birmingham, her travels and her plans. Zoe relaxed, half-listening to the gentle murmur of conversation, her eyes resting on the far blue sea horizon and the soft blue-green skyline of the mountains on the coast ahead, letting her mind drift with the flowing water and the gentle undulation of the boat. Perfect, she thought, this is perfect!

Vassily dropped anchor in the little bay and people started to prepare for the first snorkelling session. He led a small group of beginners over to one side of the bay and off they went, Sarah included. Zoe waited, carefully watching and trying on her mask. Slowly, slowly she climbed down the ladder, nervous about dropping a flipper, had it been a mistake to try to use them as well as the snorkel?   They felt huge, handicapping her feet as she dropped into the not-particularly-warm sea and clung to the last rung of the ladder. She washed out her mask and prepared to put it on. 'Wet your hair and push it off your face!' shouted Fabio quickly. And miraculously, the mask sealed itself perfectly onto her face and she gently lowered her face into the water before she could think about it. The nose guard was preventing her from inhaling any water and she could see everything perfectly through the clear glass screen. She clamped the snorkel firmly in her mouth with her teeth and set off, gliding almost effortlessly through the water with her flippers and hearing her own breathing creating a slow, steady reassuring rhythm in her ears, and her mind immediately focused on the strong, sibilant sound, her body slipping easily into the calm focused movements just like yoga. It was an extraordinary meditation, she was entering another world. The sea was so clear that she could see the sea-bed, a rocky and grassy landscape fifteen metres below her, and observe the fish flitting unafraid below her. Was this what hang-gliding might feel like?

She looked round and saw Fabio coming towards her, explaining that he was going to look for octopus, would she like to see him catch one? Zoe nodded vigorously. In a second, he had plunged down to the sea-bed, lifted a rock, made a swift grabbing movement with his hands and swam back up to the surface with his hands carefully closed. He let her have a peek at the small soft freckled brown creature nestled in his hands and then swam back to the boat and placed it gently in the aquarium.

Zoe was so excited she had forgotten all about the rest of the group. She paddled over to see how Sarah was getting on, surprised to have so easily slipped away into another world. 'I was ok, I saw you were just near us, with Vassily. He showed us the red mullet and you held the sea urchin.' Do I have an avatar? wondered Zoe, mystified. Peering short-sightedly through her goggles at a blurry figure on the edge of the group, Sarah had assumed it was her mother. Much laughter. It was a classic Sarah incident. As a small child, fascinated by the lure of the chocolate displays and too little to see beyond waist level in the crowd, she followed a familiar-looking white mac around Cadbury World right to the exit before she realised the woman wearing it was not her mother. On the car ferry to France she has also got detached from Zoe, but remembering parental instructions, with great aplomb asked the Pursar to 'ring up Mummy'; she was quite disgruntled at not being allowed to make the Tannoy announcement herself.

The healing power of laughter over shared memories ... Sarah was working too hard, Zoe thought ...

Vassily was patiently helping Eva with her mask, but clearly she was unable to manage the snorkel and he guided her gently back to the boat with her friend. 'She has early stage Alzheimer's', Sarah whispered to me, 'They are taking her with them on holiday so her husband can have a break. They are all staying in a big villa together.' Zoe thought of her own mother and their holiday in South Africa, her mother's pleasure in the world-famous gardens at Stellenbosch and the wine-tasting at the old French Huguenot wine estates, the visit to Mandela's cell on Robben Island, just before her mind started to cloud over. Here in the sunshine, gently rocking in the flat-bottomed boat, Eva was relaxed and chatty with her. Zoe explained her nervousness about the snorkelling earlier. 'But you're a natural!' she replied, and Zoe realised it was so. Returning confidence of childhood sea swimming, long carefree absent-minded days without a plan, doing exactly what you please ... a weight so huge she no longer noticed she was carrying it was beginning to lift from her shoulders ...

Vassily showed them a giant clam on the sea-bed and, nearby, some Italian mines from World War II. Back in the boat, Zoe heard him explaining how the islanders had experienced invasions and piracy, World War II and successive occupations, followed by Civil War and then the cataclysmic earthquake of 1953, which caused 75% of the inhabitants of Kefalonia to leave for Australia and the United States, in the time of his grandfather. Fabio's great-uncle had walked back to his home town in Northern Italy at the end of the war, a journey which took him two months. Two generations later, Zoe was struck by the determination of these two young men to stay in Kefalonia and find a way to make a living from the curious tourists now arriving in the unspoilt north of the island, giving new life to a 70-year-old boat and educating the visitors about the preservation of the marine environment, making it possible to experience the world of the sea creatures on their own terms, as a privileged visitor to their world. It seemed a kind of regeneration and a harbinger of hope, a new generation with a vision of co-existence of human and animal worlds, a practical understanding of their interdependence, their need for each other in order to survive.

'An octopus has 3 hearts and 9 brains …' Fabio was saying. 'One brain to control each of the 8 legs, so they can all move independently, plus one controlling the body. They can lose a leg and grow a new one without pain. The octopus lives for about 18 months and the adult is more intelligent than a dog, more like a human 2-year-old. They have evolved without a shell, so they live under stones on the sea-bed. The female builds a nest for her eggs to protect the tiny developing octopi. She stays there and can eat some of her own legs for food if necessary. When they are ready, she will release them; there will be 5000 tiny octopi from one nest and then the mother will die.' What on earth goes on in the mind of an octopus?' mused Zoe. 'What is it thinking?' Her own mind spun into a kind of reverie and then back to the talk. 'So how does he move so fast? The octopus moves about by sucking in water through his spout and then squirting it out to propel himself along.' Mesmerised, we leant over the makeshift aquarium and watched the small, delicate creature curl up in the corner and then shoot across the floor of the tank as soon as a hand loomed near. Naked and vulnerable, without any-where to hide, the soft brown body was all too visible against the smooth white floor of the tank. 'It must be very stressed' … she found herself speaking her thought aloud. After a few minutes, Fabio released it back into the sea. 'I will never eat octopus again', thought Zoe.

A little chilly, they sunned themselves on the prow of the boat, entering the second bay. They were all looking forward to seeing turtles here. Fabio described the successful conservation projects providing protected nesting sites around the island. There was nothing to be seen until Vassily cut the engine and gradually some curious scaly reptilian heads popped up a few metres away, swimming around the rocks, scavenging the debris from the fish farm. The children squealed with excitement and as they came nearer, Zoe was surprised by their size, large shells almost hidden under the water, and was quite glad they were not going to go into the sea with them. Lumbering and clumsy on land, they were swift and agile in the water, and although generally friendly, could bite if scared. Safe in the ingenious human protective shell of the boat, she was nonetheless becoming acutely aware of the vulnerability of humans should they be pitched out of their natural element into the sea. The extraordinary diversity of adaptations of the sea creatures had captured her imagination; humans appeared more and more to be a strange anomaly in this harmonious system ...

'Are you swimming?' a voice broke into her reverie. Vassily had moored the boat and 'helped' Sarah jump into the water. Zoe decided to follow. Looking down through her mask, now an old friend, Zoe was amazed this time by the sharp drop from the shoreline down into a deep shadowy moon crater under the sea. She swam over the edge ... it was cold there and she could no longer see the bottom, a lunar landscape apparently without any inhabitants. It was good to return to the warm shallows by the beach and bask in the sun, lizard-like, while she dried off and warmed up, chatting to the children. Back in the boat, Fabio offered to take her mask for her and she playfully snatched it away. 'I'm not giving this back!' she laughed, 'I want one!' 'Just make sure it's a Cressi, then' he replied with utmost professional seriousness and a pleased smile. 'Who knew?' she thought. Zoe was loving her snorkelling adventure.

'And now, who would like a glass of wine?' asked Vassily. The boat had reached the last bay and it was time for lunch. Ravenous from the swims in the cool sea, they filled their plates with feta salad, small tangy black olives, thick slices of fresh white bread and cake and sprawled out on the deck in the sun to rest. This would be their last snorkelling experience, the opportunity to visit a wreck, a small ship which had sunk there about 40 years before. 'Find the end of the mast and then follow it back to the ship', instructed Fabio. 'It is a bit …' and his English failed him. 'Spooky!' we supplied. Zoe was intrigued. The sea was so clear that it was easy to locate the mast and soon she was floating over the remains of the deck and the engine, great hulks of metal gradually losing their outline as they became of one colour with the sea-bed. She felt the thrill of investigating the sunken ship, passing to and fro over the hull, and then a sudden chill of passing over a graveyard, a ghostly place where no fish swam, a reminder of the power and treachery of the Ionian sea. Ithaca, mythical home of Odysseus, eternal traveller of these perilous seas, just across the channel. 'Heureux qui comme Ulysse, apres un long voyage …' Opera with Jess at the Roundhouse … She paddled swiftly back to the warmth of the shallow waters, the shoals of tiny fish and the rest of the group chatting and laughing on the pebble beach.

Three Rucksacks

Your rucksack is big and blue
With lots of compartments
To put in everything
For a whole weekend
It's really heavy
I ask what's in it?

My rucksack is small and grey
Two minimal compartments
Light and light-hearted
It was a gift
Surely I can squeeze in there
Everything I need?

And you have no rucksack
Share my sun lotion
Slip my old tee shirt over your bikini
Instead of beach towels
Aphrodite's biscuits
Food of the gods

Lucy swimming

Coming home from Ithaca
Hand on the ladder I turn to look back
Boat moored and waiting
Plenty of time still

Dark hair piled up
Abundant and beautiful
Swan neck and
Smiling face carefully held up out of the water

You swim gently
Paddling towards me
Confidence building
And I recall

You are the one who
When I looked down from the gallery
Made circle arms and legs for the teacher
But from above I could see something different
Ballerina on pointe
One leg and one toe
Touching the bottom

Now just you paddling
Behind you white pebble beach
Wind-dimpled sea lagoon

Cool blue topaz water
From the old olive grove
Curious brown Greek goats
Watch as we leave

Palimpsest

They reached the meeting point in good time, with a mutual sense of triumph and relief at negotiating the tight bends and vertiginous drops of the coast road successfully together in the unfamiliar hire car. It was the second week of the holiday and they were venturing further afield now. Today it was Zoe's turn to decide what to do. She had chosen a Jeep excursion over the mountains of the interior.

Their Jeep was a vintage model Zoe recognised from 40 years ago and she hopped up happily onto the side-facing seats at the rear. Glancing at her seat-belt, she realised that the lock was broken. 'Don't worry!' the driver grinned broadly, 'that won't help you.' Looking down at the dry rocks of the riverbed hundreds of feet below as he skilfully navigated the hairpins on the unmade rubble surface of the track, she saw his point.

Bumping across the parched stony plateau of the high pastures, where the streams were empty this year and few goats now grazed, they reached the ghost village. The guide explained. 'The old villages were built up here, high above those new seaside villas, to protect the inhabitants from attack by marauding pirates and invaders. When the earthquake came, fortunately it struck at midday. Almost all the villagers were out in the fields, so very few of them died, but the devastation was such that most left the island and never came back.'

Zoe wandered through the overgrown streets and observed how quickly nature had reclaimed its territory; green ferns and young trees flourished inside roofless traditional stone houses not much older than herself. 'Pompei in Kefalonia' she mused and then almost walked into an older couple, chatting to the guide in a small walled enclosure. They were 'returners', come back to find the half-forgotten houses of their childhood. The husband showed us the old stone bread oven where his mother had been standing when the earthquake demolished the rest of the house. Sarah wandered entranced through the green tunnels of the old village lanes. Zoe rested, basking in the sun on the river wall with the lizards, warming and charging their cool bodies with the sun's fierce energy. Watching her tall inquisitive child lost in thought amongst the ruined buildings she felt a surge of great affection and contentment.

'A Captain Corelli moment', she murmured, and the guide smiled. 'Which one? The real man, we know so little about. The protagonist of the novel? The hero of the film?' He smiled. They chatted amiably about truth and fiction. This place held so many stories. She gazed across the channel to nearby Ithaca. Some said that long ago the two islands had been one. Perhaps they had already been in Ulysees' ancient kingdom all this time?

Second Week

Fiskardo harbour
We sit on the quayside
Amongst the yachts
Lights shining in the dark water
Huge low full moon looking over your shoulder
I introduce you
The large and competent waitress
Looks again and laughs at the exchange of daughters
We share a big sea-bass
Sweet and juicy
Relaxed and sleepy
From our late afternoon sea-swimming
Does the moon rise and set ? I ask
We laugh we don't know the answer
We make up mantras
I am enjoying my life I say
And you
My physical things are getting better
I am happy
The sea-water full of its own medicines
Heals the skin and holds up the body
Floating weightless suspended between earth and sky
The fierce Greek sun burns away
The inflammation of the long winter
The rough pebble shingle pumices our feet
We will rise beautiful from the waves like
Aphrodite

On our way home you take my arm
I am trying very hard you say
I know it
And I feel
There can be moments
When there are miracles

Old Age

Early morning
Before anyone else is here
We are on the beach
Camped under one of the ancient olive trees
Its twisted hollowed trunk providing
Pigeon-holes where we stow our clothes
And hide our picnic from the sun
Behind us up at the road
The old-style family taverna door opens quietly
A very old Greek woman
In her neat black bathing costume
Makes her way with great dignity
Down to the sea
Slips in the water soundlessly
And swims across the little bay
I want that to be me

Part 3
κρῐ́σῐς 'Decision'

When Something is Wrong

When something is wrong, when a bone is broken
For some time there is no pain
The mind is rushing around finding solutions
Adrenalin is high body moving searching for the place
   of safety
And then
Sitting looking out into the
Unaware unchanged garden
The mind is still
Feels the wound very very gingerly
Like the tip of the child's tongue
Exploring the strange hole where
There used to be a tooth

Jacob and the Angel

Jacob wrestled with the angel all night
And nobody won
Hip dislocated
Where the angel touched him
Jacob obtains
A blessing

In the morning
Limping he knows
It wasn't a dream

We also wrestled you and I equals
And you disappeared
My hand is bruised but
It doesn't hurt and now
I too receive
A blessing

In the morning
I wake and know
It wasn't a dream

Nightmare

I was lured into a house
It seemed that girls from the office were there
They were hurting me
How? I ask softly
They were tattooing me
I had tattoos
I ran away but more women arrived
It seemed my French manager was one of them
The one that you like?
Yes
With chains to stop me escaping[*]

---

[*] Coerce: 'to restrain or dominate by nullifying individual will';
related to * incarcerate 'shut up, enclose'

Painkillers

Take 2 cocodamol 4 times a day
6 hours apart (minimum 4 hours)
2 before bed
Before you feel pain
Before your leg hurts
Or it will be too late
To get on top of the pain

I don't like medication
I rarely even use paracetamol
The consultant says I have a 'robust attitude to pain'
I take the tablets as instructed
I don't feel any pain
I don't feel anything
Vaguely I am aware of a dull ache
Somewhere between my eyebrows
My head is ridiculously heavy and
I can't remember what I am trying to do
Words are missing from my messages
I make a list and read it again
I count the tablets to check
Did I take the last two or not ?

I take the tablets
After lunch I cannot hold up my head
I lie down and I am unconscious
I am out for hours
My friend has called

She knocked on the door shouted phoned me 15 times
  but I
Don't hear a thing

We chat and eat some nuts
Nothing tastes good and I am not hungry
No pain I say
Then realise
I have felt nothing in days
Disconnected
I move my body around as if it belongs to
Somebody else
I feel a bereavement
The person I've lost
Is myself
Please reconnect me
Pain is ok
If I can feel joy

This morning
I wake light-headed
Huge relief that tablets
Are finished
I move my body around and I am back
Inside it again
I sit in the garden
The cat is heavy with sleep on my legs
Flexing her sharp claws into my skin
My mind is alert
And I see that
A week has gone by.

---

* Friends on anti-depressants tell me this is how it feels

The Augean Stables

I am like Hercules after his labour
The Augean stables are clean
And I can rest
Until the next time
I did not want to stoop to work unworthy
Clearly I am not an immortal but
I have so many qualifications and skills and this is not
   my job
I was not happy working out how to sort out
Years of neglect and dust and cobwebs
I complained a lot (not very heroic)
I binned a lot (ungraciously)
Then like Hercules diverting the mighty river
I unleashed my powerful Miele
Effortlessly cleansing everything in its path
There was a lot of argument and no reward
Except the satisfaction of the seemingly impossible
   labour completed
Fish fingers, mashed potato and a DVD

---

* The fifth labour of Hercules was to clean the stables of King
Augeas in a single day. The king had three thousand cattle and their
stables had not been cleaned for many years. It was a demeaning
task for such a hero. The king promised to give one-tenth of his
cattle as a reward. Hercules tore a hole in the foundations on one
side of the stables and directed the streams that flowed nearby so
that they washed away the filth through another opening. In this
way he accomplished the task without doing work unworthy of an
immortal. Augeas sent Hercules away without any reward.

Part 4

Reset

Cocooning

I am cocooning
I am spinning a silken pod
To protect me from harm
I will dangle from this tree
Minute soft green astronaut
On my strong tensile thread
Spinning
Spinning
Inside my cocoon
What is happening?
Disbelief
Fear
Anger
Acceptance
Grief
How long will I be inside?
I am dissolving
Forming re-forming
Lose touch with the world outside

When I emerge
Vulnerable
Wings still wet and soft
How will it be out there?
The same but not the same
In the blink of an eye the whole
Planet has been reset

Ark

We float on the waters
In our tiny ark
Just Cattie and me
Safe inside
But we can't stay here forever
We're looking for a rainbow
A dove with an olive branch
A sighting of
Mount Ararat

The Imperfect Orange

The orange is a bit old and tired
Not a perfect sphere now
A bit flattened at the North Pole
Skin a bit dull and some wrinkles
A bit like me I think and
Grin to myself

Formerly I might have
Looked askance at it
But now
I eat it eagerly
These days we are not taking
Oranges for granted

The Tipping Point

So 'only' 20 people have died in Australia
A billion creatures have been killed
An area the size of Scotland is still burning
So intensely it is generating flashes of lightening
I wonder
Is this the extreme event
That will finally turn public opinion
The apocalypse that we need to see
The tipping point?
Fake news is being spread
It was caused by arsonists
It's a freak accident
Not an environmental catastrophe
Nothing to do with neglect greed unregulated industries
Nothing to do with this so-called
Climate change phenomenon
But maybe this burning out of control vision of hell
Maybe walking through the ashes of a
Once beautiful eco-system
Maybe the eyes of the world will not
Look away this time
Maybe, just maybe this
Will be the tipping point?

---

[*] I wrote this just before the start of the coronavirus pandemic

Coming Home

Just back from India with its warmth and humanity
I am a foreigner in my own cold and miserable country
Buy my ticket from the self-service awkward machines
I have to stoop to see the keyboard to type in my pin
    number
That's because they are designed to be accessible to
    wheelchair users
M & S Coventry station so many breakfast choices
All 0% fat yoghurt though
It's what everyone wants now so it's what we order
Finally find one small pot of Greek-style full fat
    yoghurt
Only automated self-service tills
I look around I'm in no hurry
See a young assistant and tell him
I don't use those
He laughs and takes me to a carefully-concealed
    old-style till
I'm not going to either I add for good measure
He laughs again good-humouredly
There are free spoons over there he points out helpfully
That's great I say noting that they are biodegradable
    wooden ones
The notice says *Please take only what you need (?!)*
No problem with the ticket scanner
Not at this end
But at the other end it doesn't work *Why not?*

We are delayed a minute my friend says
I think we've just missed the bus
* * * * *!*

Then we see it's still there engine idling
Do you mind running for it?
And me *I'd love to run nothing better than running*
Free from all this alienating techno-nightmare
Long legs happy like a horse I sprint across the square
Jump onto the bus with the genial smiling driver
Climb up to the top deck just like when we were at
   school
Pick out the familiar streets from our elevated vantage
   point
Press the bright red bell to stop hurtle down the stairs
Our laughing driver calls out *You have a good day
   girls!*
Even though we're sixty
And I think back to earlier
No human interaction
Slowly we are eliminating
All the random joy of life

Reset

Words are flowing out like endless rain into a paper cup ...

It isn't late and I could have a good night's sleep but instead I am scribbling on an unread copy of the Big Issue which is lying around in the kitchen. Why is it that I write so much more easily cramming my words into the white spaces between the typeface, turning the magazine round to use the margins around the images, turning to a new pages as more ideas flow through my mind and demand to be released onto the paper?

I am like a small child I want to shout stamp cry be consoled

I am blaming my daughter who said yes do that and my other daughter who should have said no don't do that why didn't someone help me I am feeling so distressed at the thought of losing those photographic mementos of the joyful moments in our three-cornered wheel-off-the-bus family life before I have managed to create an album to share. I hear the disembodied voice of the Canadian woman historian on Desert Island Discs 'there will be nothing for future historians to study, no letters, no photos, no memos, does anyone even keep a diary any more? ...'

I can check my photos are in the Cloud. I start up my laptop it is very slow now and the old fear is curdling in my stomach I can't see my recent photos I remember that is the wrong Cloud I google the right Cloud but now I need to put in my password and there is the cold curdling feeling in my brain I can't remember it and everything is disintegrating I have created an IT monster and can't navigate through the mad dysfunctional labyrinth I have made my passwords are all stored on my phone whose normally friendly and helpful neat little face is blank and dark and cannot help me and the circularity would be funny if I could relocate my sense of humour.

I revert to my routines, like the cat. I sort out my washing into the yellow basket (whites) and the green basket (colours). I strip my bed and put the sheets into the machine. I fold and put away the clean towels and sheets on the drier. I empty the dishwasher and hide the used breakfast mugs and bowls inside and close the door. I sneak out into the garden in my pjs and empty the non-recyclable rubbish into the green wheelie-bin, the recyclable into the blue bin, the food waste I put outside the back door ... I will do that later in case my neighbours see me in the drive and think I am losing it.

I google a phone repair shop in the city centre. They recover phone data in almost all cases. The man on the phone is polite and reassuring. I can walk there and throw myself on their mercy. I am hot and sweaty and feel like I did after finals exams, when my exhausted brain had to work harder than it could work. It is an out of body experience. I have forgotten to breathe again.

I get in the shower and gradually as the water flows over my skin I return to my body... I am hungry and as ever the question of what to eat becomes paramount. Pate sandwich (what happens if you eat too much pate?) then packing up my smart rucksack from Euston station I don my Italian mac in case of rain and my favourite black suede shoes and I am back in myself again. I set off, reassured by the strong steady pace of my legs, striding out, I will get help.

I am walking across the park and resting my eyes on the row of huge old trees ... must have been here about a hundred years, their graceful bodies fingers almost touching I feel they are supporting me, their energy is infusing my body too. The footbridge lifts me up over the railway on its graceful arc, its bright tags and graffiti an outdoor art installation gladdening my eyes. And then down into the underpass to the city centre, stained grey tarmac and broken white tiling, the rough sleepers have been moved on today and I feel a surge of relief at not having to pass by, conscience uneasy, mumbling a greeting. The left-behind city centre, concrete blocks boarded-up businesses pawnbrokers too many charity shops and coffee bars, why is the 1950s precinct pavement always grimy, filthy, spattered with white chewing gum like lichen circles? I feel the habitual rush of love and loathing for my home city, ugly, jarring, challenging. This is no elegant white Regency spa parade, but there is a deep attachment, an umbilical cord I know I will never be able to sever. All these humans, extraordinary mix from all over the world, why are you here I silently ask them, what is your story? Sometimes there is a face I recognise from the refugee centre, an answer, sometimes I am guessing and making up stories as I pass by …

I feel a rush of air and hum of tyres passing within an inch of my body. An arrogant helmeted figure in dark shorts scythes through the aimless sprinkling of ill-dressed pedestrians. So there are Uber bikes now too I am incensed if I had stepped out of my trajectory would I have been mown down by that weaponised bike? Things are not themselves today, everything is Other or is it Uber I can't tell. I am short of sleep, reacting from an unstable place, feeling alienated from the everyday things going on around me. I am Selin from our book group text, struggling to process. The book is called 'The Idiot' I must read Dostoevsky … All about a writer who can't make sense of scenes of everyday life …

I catch sight of an overweight girl dressed in black back against the wall she is surrounded by a circle of young men are they harassing her? does she need help? then I see each of them is engrossed in his phone and the girl is too it is like another installation about non-communication all present and simultaneously all absent why do I even want a mobile?

It seems that everywhere I look there are faces passing each other without eyes meeting, no smiles, no greeting, heads down focused on the little face of their phone. I am the only one looking into the human faces and my behaviour is aberrant, for a moment I feel quite mad. I dive into a phone shop and immerse myself in the crowd of customers, gazing at the display and fending off the first assistant while I think what I exactly I want to say.

The second has a calm and unhurried approach and I decide to blurt out the whole of my predicament and tell him exactly what I need. He is listening carefully and works out solutions, I feel exhausted and struggle to concentrate and focus on the range of options, keep repeating robotically that I need to save my data. He is a flexitarian. I can save £100 by changing networks, so it's worth a bit of messing around at home isn't it? Frankly, I would rather pay the £100, I want to say, but don't want to lose face and sound incompetent. My old phone is on supercharge and is back like Lazarus from the dead, its blank face lit up again with its familiar expression, a reassuring iconic smile. I have a new phone, just like the old phone. My digital trace essence is 'migrating'. Migration will take some time, not exactly sure how long. Too many things are already transitioning, I want to say, images of my past into my future, the old ways into the new Uberworld, my mind and body into their seventh decade ...

I can go now. Two hours to kill until the process is complete. A tidal wave of relief lifts me into the bookshop opposite, with its smell of new paperbacks and carefully arranged shelves, a warm and friendly haven. I buy a newly-arrived pristine hardback copy of *It's Not About the Burqa*, the assistant smiles and is very enthusiastic about the book, and I feel back in my element like a fish thrown back into water. I am tremendously hungry! Upstairs in the café with my tea and Bakewell slice I settle in a window seat; feels like my luck is changing.

All around are people chatting and overseas students peacefully absorbed in tasks on their pastel-coloured notebooks. For more than an hour I am lost in bookworld, soothed by the friendly typeface and the comforting turning of pages, surrounded by people but oblivious. Late in the afternoon I tear myself away and collect my new phone.

Entitlement

My coat on the pub chair beside my new friend
I don't know anyone else
The latecomer says *Maybe you*
Could sit at the other table?
And my friend can sit by me.
A deep inhalation
Everyone waiting
Cats' eyes lock and measure each other
My voice says softly *You know*
I think I'd like to stay here

Part 5

Daughters

Birthday Spa

On Sunday mornings I lie in bed, my body luxuriating in the warm sea of semi-sleep, floating weightlessly between consciousness and oblivion. This Sunday I do not wake feeling rested, my body is tense, it is too early and I get up feeling a reluctance to go anywhere. It's the wrong day for this. I can tell there is no sun today no brightness just a dull grey light seeping round the edges of the blind. I am childishly disappointed by the greyness, for the first time we won't be able to be outside, there is no birdsong, the wind is cold and loud and almost horizontal, I can see it bending the garden trees and the birds are nowhere to be seen.

Radio 4 breaks into my trance ... Shamima Begum is still in the refugee camp and her baby has died of pneumonia my eyes fill I am on the edge of tears this morning, the weakness of fatigue. I can do nothing about this so to ease the sadness I say a blessing for them both ... another voice 'We don't want her back here causing trouble dividing our community' ... not a far-right zealot but a young British Muslim ... The voice moves on to discuss the modern phenomenon of loneliness. I do not feel lonely, so many friends and activities ... but I miss Paul, the one person who knew me and understood me and all about my life. That's ok, I muse, that still happens now and again, even after twenty years, unexpected and yet unsurprising.

Perhaps there will be the comforting ancient prayers or familiar hymns next? I still love the hushed atmosphere of churches and cathedrals, the contact with the other-worldly, the lingering smell of snuffed candles and incense the voices of the choir interweaving in the huge vaulted spaces and the subdued light filtering through the stained-glass, but nowadays I go there alone in moments when I need the stillness and the inner calm.

This Sunday the hymns are dirge-like and I am not in the right frame of mind for Lent today so I switch off the radio and go down to see the cat. I struggle to make tea the kettle is definitely leaking and unsafe so I use an old saucepan feeling unreasonably aggrieved at the minor inconvenience. I begin to coax the reluctant body back into life it seems all I am depends on a cup of tea and a few pieces of fruit.

Some glimpses of blue appear behind the wet greyness and I have a plan. I will get there early and walk around the box-hedged hill-top gardens and king-of-the castle views across the low-lying meadows below. In half an hour I am there, astonished at my own earliness; there is a ping on my phone and 'I can see you !' and there is Clare, just across the car-park, thinking to surprise me and laughing at both of us. She gets out of her car, sorting her bag out with difficulty, fragile but determined and we fall into step easily with few words, braced against the cold wind beating against our faces. Slipping into the walled garden under the espaliered cherry trees with a few blossoms still lingering, we cross the lawn to the wide paved terrace and the sublime almost feudal views, noticing the new houses across the fields below creeping towards the foot of the hill.

It is time to go in and there is a primitive sigh of the body hyper-aware of entering the warm building, letting go of the battle against the exhilarating freezing wind. We are in the spa and all is tranquillity, harmony and soothing surroundings, warm water lapping gently at the pool steps, light breaking through the clouds and striking the iridescent blues of the tiny mosaic squares. Jo appears. We run outside, wet from the pool and jump into the hot jacuzzi, brave and beserk like Icelanders, shrieking and laughing in the cold wind, gazing up into the miracle of the blue above and the ancient trees. Harem-like, we are oiled, massaged, cleansed and beautified, we lie and doze gently under the magical hands of the young girls in their softly-lit and enticingly-scented little music-filled rooms. We emerge blinking like souls from another world for afternoon tea and champagne. Clare has found me hand-made earrings identical to the ones I lost some months ago; Jo has brought me marzipan calissons from the Midi and lavender savon de Marseille; I am restored.

Christmas Fair

Is this you standing there at the top of the staircase
Framed in the gallery window
Beside your little round cafe table?
It's piled high with bottles jars and
Brightly-coloured Christmas boxes
Mango strawberry vanilla coconut pumpkin
Good enough to eat
I dab some on my skin
Rub it in
Enjoy the sweet fresh aroma rising
Off my warm hands
Listen to you chatting to the passers-by
Showing them the samples
Boho-chic and just yourself in your
Short black skirt and big boots
The jewellery-maker comes by and
Buys something for her boyfriend
A yoga friend comes up to me and chats
Across the gallery a Syrian woman calls to me
Shows me exotic beaded felt Christmas stockings
Made by the refugees
I used to work with
An Indian woman holds up her throws and bangles
Her children in their best silk costumes darting through
    the crowd
Bright tiny dancers from another world
We don't have time now to look at all the other stalls

The bar is filling up fast and we are getting busy
The bar manager brings us tea and tiny spicy hot mince
    pies
The fair is going well and she would like us all to come
    back every month!
We try to look nonchalant but we are both excited
From a chance encounter with an old friend and
    colleague
You have found your niche and at last
You have flown right out of the gilded corporate cage

Fragile

Age looks at young tear-stained face lifted up to me
We are so fragile so easily dashed
Visions and dreams of how life is going to be
Impatience of youth when will I find love home
    stability?
Building up hope til it feels like certainty
Once again everything comes crashing down.

All that I know is
Pick yourself up and dreams do come true for us
But like those gnomic ancient Greek oracles
Often in ways we cannot imagine and
Least expect.

Falling in love is so hard on the knees

Christmas Party

And is this you?
Standing there on the red carpet
A crystal chandelier blazing in the gilded mirror behind
    you
Black lace dress gently clinging to tall slender figure
Long legs like the models we watched
In the square at Milan Cathedral
I peer and see a man in evening dress
Tiny distant in the glass
Beneath the high white stucco ceiling
Perhaps he is preparing his after-dinner speech
Or you with your wide smile and sense of fun
You could be the speaker
I see now in silhouette
Green feathered branches of Christmas tree
Silver candlesticks lighting (I guess) white cloths on
    dining tables
Hand on hip ringlets updo very London
You might be a snap from the Tatler
And in life you will not go unnoticed
So where are you heading now?
I wonder fascinated

I can recall a moment like this
In my mind I see myself my hair my dress but
Do not have a photograph

Gardening

Zoe had been in Birmingham all weekend helping her daughter to mow her lawn for the first time ever. There had been a few false starts. The week before they had spent a couple of hours studying mowers in Homebase and eventually found the one they wanted, only to find a huge raincloud bursting over them as they left the store. The weather had not deigned to fit in with bank holiday gardening plans.

The second attempt a week later went much better. The sun was out and the sky was blue. With a flourish, Zoe slashed open the box and prepared to get out the beautiful new mower. Clare went to check the dilapidated old shed she had inherited and found she already had a mower left behind by the previous owner and in full working order. Zoe's momentary surge of irritation was instantly mollified by the sight of her daughter's proud face as she carefully manoeuvred the machine up and down the grass. A robin appeared as soon as they finished and perched on the old apple tree and the garden was full of birdsong. Spring had arrived. Blackbirds swooped down to gather twigs and moss for a nest somewhere nearby. It seemed like a good omen for the new house.

Zoe always felt so relaxed out of doors and though she did not really know much about horticulture, she had always enjoyed digging and planting, the smell of newly-mown grass and damp earth. She was pleased to see her daughter starting to take pleasure in tending her garden too. It was a satisfying project to embark on together. Despite the inevitable hissy fits as mother and daughter adjusted themselves to working together, they had done a good job and Zoe was amused to find a photo posted on Facebook when she got home.

Part 6

India

Return to Delhi

From the taxi glimpse
Parliament and President's House
Immense imperial architecture
Lit up in the darkness
Maimed beggars slums under flyovers
Elegant New Delhi boulevards
Posters in tuc tuc
Against violence against women
Meera Syal's book the case of the Dalit girl

There are about 30 million people in Delhi
(Depending how you count them)
Lanes full of traffic and crowds in the market but
Indians are hyperaware of others' space
Not hurrying but moving fast
Cars hoot constantly
Tell each other where they are
And everyone is safe
The old man steps off the kerb
Walks through the traffic flow
The attitude of our guide
Is calm and graceful
Perhaps he is surprised at
Our expectations?

Delhi to Agra 2018: Notes from the Motorway

The sign says
Two wheeler lane
Using lanes improves safety
4 people on one motorbike
Man in jeans women in sari and pashmina
Child

Crops in fields
Rice
Sugar cane
Millet cotton mustard

Natural spring for irrigation
Brick factory with chimney
Shrine brightly painted
Take care driving Life is precious

Village school
Traditional village huts made of ? Shape like yurt
Modern village houses concrete oblongs like Africa
Pampas grasses green trees and bushes
Vegan organic farm
Bicycles and farmers walking on dikes between
    paddy fields
Farm workers men and women

Threshing floor of plastic sheeting workers bringing
sheaves, threshing by hand
Mechanised farming, tractors, ploughed fields
Overspeeding will invite prosecution

Starbucks 5 km
New temple huge delicate Moghul style built 2009 size
of new Liverpool cathedral
Cart piled with huge load pulled by farmer using
bicycle
Huge sacks transported through Old Delhi market on
men's heads and shoulders
Wholesale market businesses export all over India and
abroad

Beehives
Plastic tents for workers

Motorway 2010 Delhi – Agra
Holy cows small like herd of deer wander freely not
milking cows
Milk from buffalo ?
Yoghurt at breakfast

Accident prone zone
Pace of change
Grace of India
People, attitudes, customs remain
Namaste

Taj Mahal

Pale perfection seen from afar
Across the soft green fields of memory
Barely there in the heat haze
Exquisite marble minarets and flawless dome
Twenty years in construction
A colony drawn there
From all the known world
Thousands of craftsmen
The first assembly line in history
To sculpt and decorate this marble dream
Glimpsed now by an ageing Emperor
From his prison tower
His Empress and his life's companion dead
The guide suggests perhaps he felt some guilt
He brought her pregnant to his battle-tent
And she miscarried there and died
There was no doctor
Deposed by his own son
Only his eyes free now to travel to her memorial
For fear of treachery and usurpers
His daughters husbandless
One loved him
Was companion-prisoner to his old age
Under its walls
Myself no longer young
I place my palm against the delicate flowers of lapis
Trapped in the warm marble
And dream of a life gone by

Spice market

Up the narrow half-ruined staircase
Past men on the landing squatting grinding spices
Heaps of bright powders
Scent of garam masala
On the drying terraces
Up on the roof
Surrounded by the faded Moghul
Balustrades and crumbling courtyards
Talking about the hijra
Who used to live nearby
Behind the delicate sun-bleached fretwork shutters
Arundhati Roy's tales of Old Delhi
Shajahanabad
I can hardly believe I'm here
Look out from the Jama Masjid*
Spaghetti tangles of electric cables
Cascade over the shop fronts
Above the narrow bustling streets

---

* Great Mosque

Arriving in Goa

Beach huts in Goa
Stone's throw from the ocean
Slender pillars palm trees
Graceful ribs of branches high overhead
No-one but us
In the darkness huge crash
On my friend's hut roof
Coconut falling from far above
Tropical silver dawn over the ocean's skin
Two mugs of ginger tea
Pull on yoga top and baggy trousers
Sit in half lotus gaze on the small dark Shiva god
Pardeshi is ready to start our first practice

Rushin

Small gentle hands light touch never stop moving over
  body
Release sore muscles rub in oils soothe thirsty skin
Hut with walls of matting old-style ceiling fan cotton
  sheet for door
Couch so comfortable sea breeze flowing through the
  room
Feet in warm water reading novel soothing massage
Strong on sole of foot pain for a moment then release
  of tension
Skin scrubbed and polished until soft like a baby
Bright red Diwali nail polish on toenails
What does your name mean? I ask the girl
My name is light

Pronate

At school
I never liked my feet
Too big too wide for shoes
'You have flat feet' said the teacher unhelpfully
At university
Blissful walking around barefoot
My friend observed
'Your feet are so natural your toes so straight'
At work my officemate said
'That's very common
It's called pronate you just need stronger trainers'
At the shop the outdoors man
Puts insoles in my walking boots

And now at yoga
I am creating arches
Making my feet strong
I use my prehensile toes to hold a pencil
And write my name
And people laugh and have a go
Not everyone can do that!
Walking in the wet grass I look down
Yellow flower petals
Adorn my beautiful strong feet and I am
Proud of them at last

Yoga Retreat

Wade out of the body-warm tropical ocean
Ask *Is there anything I can*
Do with my hair?
Hairdresser friend says
Honestly? No.
So I just scrunch it
Don't even rinse it
It doesn't know and
It doesn't care

Bodies are revelling in
Release from winter clothes
Strong and so flexible in this gentle heat

All in our wide circle
Sitting cross-legged
Brass trays of thali
Balanced on our knees
Beach clothes no bras maybe no pants
Who cares?

Out on the rocks sunset meditation
Breath is so slow now slower than the sea
Inhale happiness exhale peace

Gate 13

I am at Gate 13
Where are you?
We are not at Gate 13
We are sharing fish and chips and having a last Indian
    beer in the bar
Waiting for Anj who is still in the duty free
Looking for a favourite perfume
We do not see the WhatsApp
Eventually I get up and move towards the gate
There is an immense glass hallway with a very long
    moving metal track
It looks quite far to Gate 13
I get on it with my case and am carried along
Someone is running the wrong way along the steel track
It is Jo with our tickets red-faced and anxious
I am contrite
Look back and
No-one is in sight on the shining path
I proceed to Gate 13
Our flight is boarding in orderly fashion
We are the last
Here are the tardy ones
Followed by Anj with the perfume
Asking the boarding crew
Could I just pop into the ladies please?
And I am filled with affection for my
Random yoga family

The Dog

The dog hunches on the beach back turned on me looks
    out to sea
Lifts his head and gently howls three times at the moon
I see the fine grey haze of the storm on the horizon
In a waking dream I clearly saw departing swallows
    gathering
Swirling patterns tiny specks in a soft blue sky
Alone and ill at ease I rise to go and smell
Sour winds of havoc in the humid air

The Death Card

People are terrified if they get the death card!
Says my Portuguese friend talking about the Tarot
But they don't need to be scared
It doesn't mean someone will die
It means that old things will pass away
So that something new can come into your life
I am in India looking at the Shiva god
Shiva the Destroyer[*]
In the little shrine before me in the yoga shala
Smiling and tranquil he holds up his palm towards us
Behind him the all-powerful turbulent Indian Ocean
The cyclone has just passed by lifting the roofs off our
      beach huts
Silhouettes of men perch like monkeys squatting to
      repair them
Slowly but surely our little group of travellers
Splinters and falls apart and I know
It is time now
For some new beginnings

---

[*] Shiva 'the auspicious one' is one of the three principal deities of
Hinduism; he uses his powers of destruction to make way for
beneficial change

Part 7

Home

New Chairs

I vowed I would never come here again
Daughters fractious nothing purchased
Can't find our way out of the
Labyrinth of model rooms
Everything is looking tired and worn
Or is that just me?

I sink down into a small blue cushioned chair
Can't go any further
It's rather comfortable
Welcomes me with open arms
I think I'll stay here
Just for a while

Hunger rouses me
Girls are back and urgently
Following our noses at last we find the lunch place
Meatballs in gravy smash potatoes frozen peas
Straight from the 70s
Nothing has changed

Sun comes out and I decide to leave them there
I will walk home
A few days later
I think about my chair again
Measure and calculate
Ring up and order two

A friend helps me assemble them
On goes their soft blue skin
We sink down into the sturdy cushioned nests
Chairs make a room warmer and
much more inviting
Certainly more so than rickety old rattan

Little kids curl up in them
Cat snoozes friends relax
Light the fire
Add soft blue blankets
Autumn is here and now
My room is complete.

The Pond

Today it feels propitious and in my pyjamas I go out into the garden, breathing the cool early spring air. I ought to clean the pond, I think, and yet somehow I know they are already there before me. There are the islets of black-specked minute jelly globes, there is a gentle plosh as I approach and the adult frogs dive beneath the rocks. And there, the first tadpoles wriggling, small implausible black sperm in the nutritious waters of the pond.

The Dining Room

It feels like an auspicious start to Agniezska's work on her PhD dissertation ... cold but clear, bright blue sky like spring outside, sun streaming onto the soft yellow walls of the dining room through the graceful semicircle of tall glass panes of the bay window, converging on the big beech table ... I see Lucy labouring over her master's dissertation, my godson sweating over his university application, my partner cursing as his online registration timed out ...

Friends wondered at me creating a whole room just for occasional parties and dinners but I see now its true purpose: bright airy well-proportioned and high-ceilinged space for writing, homework, exam revision, getting a new job, booking a holiday ...

A room where you can dream dreams and make your visions come true and us, always pushing up like the hyacinth bulb bursting out on the windowsill and filling the room with its scent, pushing up towards the future, bright and beckoning yet never materialising in the time, manner and place that we expect.

A Friend in the Shape of a Cat

Together we are dozing
In the small conservatory
Rain strumming on the roof makes it
Good to be inside
Familiars surround me
Along the shelf
A wedding-present blue-striped jug
My mother's old blue-painted octagonal Chinese teapot
Bamboo handle a memory lost many years ago
Little orange-painted pots from a Syrian student friend
No two the same
A small white lighthouse-shaped tin garden lantern
Five cut-out seagulls on a line of wooden mooring posts
A blue metal candlestick Matisse bird taking off
A chalky pebble full of holes from the Ile de Re
On the floor a dimpled whelk-like sculpture of a shell
Wire form with white papery skin
I'm proud of that
My first ever artistic effort in three-D
The green star of an aloe plant from my gardening
    friend from book group
The circle of an Indian paisley white and wood relief
    tray
Improvised small table for tea book pencils
Comfortably sprawled on my ancient Ikea chaise
    longue

With rug and you curled up warm in the crook of
   my leg
You immobilise me silently for an hour or two
We are now so at ease with one another
From long years together my
Friend in the shape of a cat

After the Holiday

First morning home and in my pyjamas
I slide open the glass screen of my lean-to conservatory
Instantly breathe in rose and mock-orange
Hot grass honeysuckle
Birch bark and lavender
Eye is bemused by
Jumble of new growth
Exhuberant profligate
Foxglove shoots sky-high white trace on the blue
Wading through long grass bright with pin-pricks
    yellow and pink
I reach the deep green tiny pond's
Dense fringe of mallow leaves
Under the small rock
Unblinking eye stares back
First frog of summer
All's right in my world

People in the Park

On Facebook a photo of the trees in the Memorial Park
Graceful, in full leaf, greens and copper beech
Shade and full sun
Spaces paths between
Like an arboretum
A name under each tree
My friend's post
'If I lived near this beautiful place
I would go there every day'
I do live near
I get out my bike and go there
I cycle round the outside path
Sign says 1.6 miles
Around wide open football fields and the
Saucers of the golf course
Under the spreading trees
Past the rose garden
Glimpse the white memorial and the concrete skate
    park
Pass the now closed cafe
Path sprinkled with people imbibing late afternoon sun
Cyclists crossing straight home from work
Children on first shiny bicycles not sure how to proceed
Plump young woman in pink just started running
Two sitting quietly together on a bench
Boys racing joshing shouting
Young mother with pushchair

Older man in blue shirt going the other way round
Young Asian men gesticulating chatting
Dog walkers dogs hear me first and move swiftly away
Small children dawdling and picking up little sticks
Family with picnic out on the playing field

Second lap
Woman still running a little more slowly
Blue shirt man serious still doesn't smile
Couple strolling thoughtfully underneath the trees
Walkers I recognise mainly by their dogs
The boys are at the skate park now
Rose garden sparks of so many colours
Seated women bright silk clothes
Children home-made food and picnic rugs
I will go one more time
Legs feel a little effort
Pink woman walking now blue eyes flash a smile
Dogs runners roses blur of trees and people leaving
I am pedalling gently
Out of the gate and home

La Belle au Bois Dormant*

Shut in by the falling rain
Dozing waiting for something to change
The trees and shrubs have overgrown my garden
I can hardly see out of my windows
And my rooms are dim dark subterranean green
Feverish delirious pricked by the winter virus
Endless days I wait for the lifting of the spell
This morning the tree man comes
Striding through my forest
I am awoken by the whirring of chain saws
Look up and the web of branches has all disappeared
Light floods through the garden through the open
   spaces
Winter sky bright blue cloudless like a summer's day
Sun pours
Into my eyes
Tree-man whatsapps me
Hey gorgeous has your kettle broke?
I step outside laughing with a mug of tea

---

* Sleeping Beauty

Part 8

Bubble

Christmas Day

This year there are seven of us
Maybe it's the perfect number
The three Kaplan Ladies and our
Adopted Polish family
The children five and seven
Make everything joyful special
Scurrying happily about
Bringing sauces glasses napkins
Young expectant voices
Fiona is it ready yet ?
We fly around the kitchen
Fuelled by chilled Spanish Cava
And smoked salmon canapes
Sing loudly along to the *Three Tenors* booming out
Christmas in Vienna
This year's festive soundtrack
Their father carves the venison
It smells so good and so does
The sweet red wine gravy
The children serve the vegetables
Everyone full of anticipation
And our dinner is delicious (phew !)
We heat up the brandy
Ignite the pudding mini-mountain and
The little girl
Proudly carries it in
No big presents this year

Instead dinners for homeless people at
Crisis at Christmas
But a friend has given me a toasting fork
The fire is already hot
And remembering I have some marshmallows
We spear them and roast them over the flames
Until someone calls out
The marshmallows are on fire !
One daughter is dozing now
I realise
The other has been filming us
Polish Dad is quietly reading
The history book we gave him
Polish Mum is seeing if she can
Hit the high soprano descant
We laugh at ourselves
And all agree
It has been the very best
Christmas Day for years

Cornwall

I turned my back on the two pleasant women sitting opposite me in the small fishing boat and threw up neatly and silently over the side. 'Excuse me,' I said, 'I just had to be sick.' 'Oh, we didn't even notice,' they said tactfully. 'Are you all right?'

There was a great sense of relief now that the inevitable had happened and I felt fine. 'Don't mention it to the others!' I gestured towards the two couples chatting in the bows. My Australian cousin Lucy and I had organised this trip to Fowey to spend the day with my brother and his partner Gerty and I didn't want to end the very successful outing on an awkward note.

I had got up so early to miss the traffic that I got down to Cornwall before breakfast and surprised my cousin and her husband having coffee in the old fisherman's cottage they had rented on the quayside. To book the ferry trip, Lucy had only to push up the sash window and call down to the captain directly below. The sky was blue with little cloud or wind and the sea propitious. Of course we could have walked one way as we had done two years before, six miles of spectacular views along the steep inclines of the coastal path, but Lucy was not inclined to do that again. Instead, more time for lunch and shopping. Strolling around the cobbled streets, Gerty found a soft pink jacket we persuaded her to buy.

Such a pleasure, spending a day like this with my brother, it seemed as if decades had slipped away. 'Is there anything particular I should know about her?' I had asked before our first meeting with Gerty. Laconic as ever, he replied 'Not really, she's French-speaking African-Caribbean from Guadaloupe.' 'Great!', I thought, 'We'll all speak French !' I felt somehow that we would all get on. And so it was to be.

For Julia

Sensational sparkling lady in black, looking rather nifty
We're gathered here to wish you well for now it seems
you're sixty.
When you moved here you asked us, 'Did we think that
you should try it?'
Next door to the Baraset ? 'Oh yes, 'we said, 'Just buy
it!'
Warm-hearted, open, kind and also generous to a tee
You lent us your house in Cornwall when we were all
fifty.
So many pranks at school together, really we were
shameless,
That wasn't Julia of course, she was completely
blameless.
If we fall out it's Julia who brings us all together
Samaritan-trained she's seen us through all kinds of
stormy weather.
When I went out with Farmer George she said 'See you
at the wedding!'
It soon became apparent that was not the way that
things were heading ...
And just as you think that really things cannot get any
worse
That big bad laugh rings out a peal and drowns out all
your curses.
A legendary sea-scout coach, with Julia there's no
flannel

This is a woman who can skipper you clean across the
   English Channel.
Dashing off to Oxford in your spanking black
   convertible
We were all twenty-one again, against the evidence
   which was quite incontrovertible *(eleven children
   between us!)*
With Howard there have been so very many moments
   that you cherish
Though when he threw your files into the garden some
   thought that love might perish.
Bell-ringing, singing, history, is there no end to what
   our friend can do?
Well she is only sixty so who knows? ....
I hear that you're in love again and that his name is
   Mungo??
A prize if you find a rhyme for that ... trying might be
   fun though!
Now it is time we all stand up and swiftly raise our
   glass
It's time to toast the birthday of our very own
   Warwickshire Lass!

What is in the Basement at the Museum?

I hold my breath as they go skeetering down the hard white concrete steps of the museum, boy 6 and girl 4 rebounding off the panels of the landing and hurtling down the final descent to the basement, arriving in an excited tumbling heap on the smooth tiled floor.

Mindful of older bones, I follow cautiously with the guide and the two other pleasant women, all of us filled with a rush of curiosity. We are in the intestines of the museum, the working parts, the secret spaces visitors never normally see.

Here is the loading bay, where priceless exotic treasures arrive, the Peacock Throne, the sculptures, the tapestries, the swords and shields on loan from London. Here is the huge lift in which they travel up to the exhibitions and glass cases. Stepping around the packing cases we follow the guide around the corner to a high-ceilinged-hangar big enough for a small plane. She turns a wheel like a miniature ship's capstan and two mighty walls slide back, to reveal hidden shelves from floor to ceiling.

It is a library, filled not with books, but crammed with creatures of all kinds. 'Are they dead?' checks Zosia. 'Yes, they're dead.' I do not attempt to explain taxidermy.

'How did they dead?' Hmmm, tricky … I say I do not know exactly, which is true. We gasp as Ali pulls out a shallow drawer full of big, bright, turquoise-blue and black iridescent tropical butterflies, bequeathed to the museum on condition they are not exposed to daylight. We see a tray of delicate speckled moths, cream, pink and brown like bird's eggs, native to this area.

Then to the birds. Zosia correctly names a robin and is proud. A friendly pair of Gressingham ducks are waddling towards us and a small owl sits on a stump, yellow eye fixed upon us. 'Is it alive?' checks Zosia one more time. 'It's real,' explains Gregory helpfully, 'but not alive.' The guide holds up the birds and Zosia likes the parrots, but we cannot touch these as some are preserved in arsenic. We can stroke a tiny fieldmouse. As a child I had a mouse and still recall its soft warm body in my hand and its bright eyes. Nowadays city children rarely keep small pets at home.

Zosia likes the foxes and I lift her up to see their clever russet faces and their sleek forms, a bit surprised perhaps to find themselves here. Gregory has found a crocodile (a baby one) and on the shelf behind a little alligator and a turtle. These are perfectly preserved and new, illegal imports from returning tourists, confiscated by Customs and Excise. What a joy for a small boy to get up close and personal with these scaly creatures!

And finally, a drama frozen in time. A mongoose and a snake locked in a mortal combat, probably neither will win. The strong snake coils around the mongoose's body, but its head is caught in the sharp teeth of the mongoose's mouth. Both may die. An image straight from Kipling.

The children are more interested in the turtle. Politely we are reminded we must leave now, for our half an hour is up. Reluctantly we drag ourselves away. The capstan turns, the tall shelves move together, Scylla and Charybdis, clashing rocks we must escape, or be forever trapped, new specimens in the museum.

Un Ballo in Maschera

I bump into you at the opera
Each equally surprised and smiling
You explain *It's our first time ever*
A friend gave us some tickets
Un Ballo in Maschera
And you are loving it
This is my brother and his partner
I explain to my friend
We are just stepping out of
Verdi's dark theatre of intrigue and
Misconstrued intentions
Into the bright light and laughter of the crowd

Glamping at Janet's

Arriving at the converted barn, I exclaimed in delight and surprise at how idyllic everything looked in the warm spring sunshine. I had not seen the place since mid-December. The winter had been hard for Janet. Darkness fell early, blotting out the beautiful views and the nights were cold. 'Why don't you pretend it's just a holiday?' I said. 'Nothing is forever. Wait until the summer comes!'

And now, right on cue, a late Easter and a burst of unseasonably warm weather. We sunned ourselves in the garden and watched her little boy playing with the bantams. I told her about my utter failure to convince any of my friends to go glamping with me. In response, Janet showed me a video clip of her gorgeous new orange octagonal tent. 'It's a yurt!' I cried excitedly. My delightfully off-the-wall and very determined ex-office-mate grinned. We didn't hesitate. When would the weather again be so perfect? The bank holiday mood was upon us and neither of us had any plans for the next day ...

And so it was I found myself rushing home, clambering about the attic excitedly assembling my camping gear, stumbling off to bed in a happy haze of anticipation. The next morning, the annual ritual washing, cleansing and purifying of my house ready for Easter Sunday, making sure I had the food for the family gathering in twenty-four hours' time, chocolate eggs for the children. At last, hot and tired and eager to leave the city, I packed my camping gear into the car and set off.

I found Janet, ever resourceful and bursting with energy, assembling a gazebo to provide some shade. For the little boy, I had packed my orange cylindrical ceiling duster with fronds like a strange sea-cucumber. Before long he had worked out how to extend it to its full length and reach us from afar with his tickling stick, making the adults giggle and squirm at his pleasure. No-one was safe. The garden was full of laughter.

By early evening, the sun was going down behind the almost-in-leaf trees and the low hedgerow, in streaks of soft orange and slate blue. Lungs full of cool hill-top air I set off for my tent as the light began to fade. The temperature was rapidly dropping now and I knew that despite the 22C heat of the day it would reach a low of 7C in the small hours. I got into bed fully dressed in my cotton tunic, leggings and two pairs of socks, burrowed into my sturdy three seasons sleeping bag, and arranged my feather duvet from home and Janet's hand-made patchwork quilt on top for good measure.

Switching on my mini-camping lamp, I got out my book. I had bought the lamp months ago, more in hope than in expectation, and I was childishly thrilled to be out here in the darkness reading by its steady glow. Snug and warm, I was soon drowsy after all the exertions of the day. I pulled my hoodie up around my head and fell asleep listening to the gentle sounds of ewes and lambs calling to each other and occasional cars passing far away, a muted dull crescendo and diminuendo from another world.

I wake slowly and calmly, taking in my tent-world, the fluting and warbling notes of the birds, the distinctive calls and elaborate answering trills, and a sporadic soothing chirring percussion, perhaps a woodpecker. My phone says it is five o'clock and it is barely light. Half-asleep, I stumble across the groundsheet, slip on my shoes and carefully open the ingeniously-hinged semi-circle of fabric which is the door, zipped and sealed shut overnight, and go quickly into the field and to relieve my bladder animal-like behind the hedge. I make out the giant yellow iron claw of the digger and the huge red fan of the harrow waiting at the edge of the field. Back in my cocoon, I lie and luxuriate in my unbelievably comfortable bed. I will stay here for a while and enjoy the profound stillness of my Easter morning.

I gaze around the interior of my octagonal modern yurt, so perfect! The roof is orange and its delicate ribs are flexed above me. There are windows in every side of the octagon and daylight is permeating through, illuminating the soft bright colours all around me. A riot of turquoise, yellow, orange, green and red patterned squares cover my double bed: one of Janet's own hand-made quilts. Bright stripes of orange, pink and yellow glow on the rag rug, under a small wooden chair and table with a green storm lantern. I have a patterned beaker and a bottle of water, a green canvas half-moon cupboard, a tiny turquoise folding bedside table for my book and phone. Ever-resourceful, Janet has raised my mattress off the ground on two old wooden pallets from the farm and I am warm as toast.

Experimentally I form small clouds with my breath as I emerge, but I can feel the sun warming my back already. I have slept for almost eight hours, like the animals and birds, from dusk until first light. Away from the stuffy central heating my head has cleared and I am recalibrated to a natural circadian rhythm. My body is at ease, I feel restored and I am full of glee, because I have gone glamping after all.

'Fam'

Like a scene from *Friends*
All talk at once interrupting telling stories
Cracking jokes
Ciao la Mama!
Italian boy sweeps me off my feet in a huge hug
I am a part of the teasing and the banter
Talking of yoga headstands and India
Someone lost it on the plane! And I said
'You can say anything you like to me because...
...because you're dead to me! you don't exist!'
Egyptian boy deadpans dramatically
Laughter bursts out surprise release relief
Italian *It's just been too long since ...*
Laughter again updates requested
Did you pull that girl what happened ?
Chat with Spanish girl flamenco in Seville
A children's educational project in Africa
Daughter's Dutch flatmate across the table
Catches my eye smiling shy much younger quieter
Enjoys the repartee
Perfecting his already near-perfect English
Careful and professional he is our waiter
I used to do this for a job
Sorry! Sorry! Sorry!
Just in time here is Lucy
Bringing beautiful yellow and red roses
Chloe has made a surprise for the dessert

It's a piping hot bakewell pudding!
Oohs! and *Aahs!* around the table
It smells delicious!
Replete now tipsy contented
Yes we will have some more!

Part 9
Stories

The Coventry Archive

I look around the archive room at the museum and think, how fond I have become of all these people in just one year. The museum staff have organised a talk for the creative writing group from the Resource Centre for the Blind, and there is great excitement and anticipation. Each person now has an item from the archives to examine.

Hilda sits next to me, at ninety-eight, queen in her wheelchair, the 1940s winter white fox fur sets off her neat white-blonde curls and graceful profile. 'You wore it over one shoulder, like this,' and I see the smart wartime city girl. 'I saved for months to buy something like this.' Forgotten the fall, wrist fracture, stick, the loneliness of the long-lived, the visits of the green and orange people no sooner glimpsed than disappearing, constructions of a mind struggling with confused messages of malfunctioning optic nerves.[*] Last week that sharp mind dictated an entire short story in precise cool tones, a murder mystery in a dilapidated country house, our very own 'Agatha Christie.'

---

[*] 'Charles Bonnet syndrome causes a person whose vision has started to deteriorate to see things that are not real (hallucinations). These may be simple patterns, or detailed images of events, people or places. They are only visual and do not involve hearing things or any other sensations. ' www.nhs.uk

Two years younger, Barbara leans forward in her chair, soft pink quilted jacket, ever practical, bright blue eyes examining the A3 prints of the first bicycles made here, the motor cycles and the cars. 'Where were these made?' she asks, pointing out the fragile sidecars woven of cane like great big baskets for the passengers to sit in. 'I think they used to weave the cane and silk too out at Ryton-on-Dunsmore.' Recorded on her dictaphone, leaving the Yorkshire mills to join the war effort in Coventry, winding cloth onto the struts of the bombers, one of the first women in the factory and in the whole country to be trained for this job.

A young'un (mid-forties) Ali shows me a book of pre-war photos of his home town, Kenilworth, scrutinising the images with his powerful glasses ... what he can recognise ? We see the little cinema long gone. He turns to question me and I'm alarmed by the huge eyes that stare at me, refracted by his lenses. What will he write about this trip next week ? I wonder.

James, another young'un, holds a small paper bag from the shop. 'Postcards', he confides and we look at them together. *The Fury*, an Expressionist painting like Munch's 'Scream', strong black park railings on bright green, high curving wall, a knot of agitated faces running towards us out of the frame; a mediaeval tapestry, deep reds and blues. Why has he chosen these ? I wonder ... he tells me the bright colours caught his eye. His story is a bloody pirate sea-battle over buried treasure.

George, ageless, chipper with his neat white beard, ever curious, grasps the cylindrical bellows of the vacuum cleaner and feels its long metal snout, ant-eater-like, suck up the dust. Will this appear transmogrified in his ongoing sci-fi tale of Trump and Putin meeting on the Moon, as he is deep in background technical research. So far, much to my disappointment, he has stalwartly resisted my suggestion to write in a female double agent, James-Bond-style love interest of deadly duplicity.

'We sprinkled tea-leaves on the rugs to catch the dust !' says Dorothy, new to the group, diffident but delighted to be part of things. I place the soft white capsule in the palm of her hand: a silk worm's cocoon. Once they were delivered to the Cash's ribbon factory. Something knocks inside. Is it still alive ? she asks, then laughs … it's a long time since Cash's closed. She is just getting started on her memoirs.

Here is Edwina, an inspiration at seventy, and I lean in close to speak. She's laughing as I place the soft fox fur on her shoulders, courageous and vivacious, facing loss of hearing and of sight. Perhaps the most prolific writer of them all, she gave a poem to us all last week, to celebrate the joy of Easter, from darkness into light … She hugs me. 'Ooh, I love all this ! There's such a buzz !'

Now Doreen, giggling about her family tripping over her white stick, brown eyes wide with pleasure, at ninety-seven regales the archivist with stories of the top shops and the watch-makers, sent at eight or nine to deliver the tiny watch-springs, climbing up the stairs to the wide-windowed workshops level with the chimney pots and filled with light. She has a degree in stage design. Her first love was a German prisoner of war.

Here, full of tales of bygone days in Coventry, they are our audio-books, a living archive. As we leave, preoccupied with manoeuvring wheelchairs, long white sticks navigating narrow spaces and glass cases of the gift shop, the manager appears beside me silently and hands me my mac and scarf and the umbrella I left yesterday.

Twenty-something

We moulded to each other
You and I
As only twenty-somethings can
Only half-formed
Surprising ourselves and each other
Knowing we would not part
Whatever harsh words were spoken
In the heat of the moment

Reading *Becoming* by Michelle Obama

Zoe is reading Michelle Obama's story at the point where she meets her future husband. Focused on her career at a top legal practice in Chicago, Michelle is taking a break from dating. She falls into a pleasant working relationship with her new mentee, gradually developing into a friendship based on the fact that they are two African-Americans with a desire to change the status quo in a firm where only four out of five hundred lawyers are black. She notes his tall lanky figure and slightly geeky clothes, and his mind continually working on huge cerebral socio-political problems, such as how to reduce income inequality, while she is content to enjoy her after-work happy hour in the bar relaxing with her hard-working young professional friends.

Putting the book down, Zoe sees Paul as she first met him, in the graduate common room. He is tall and dark and has a halo of tightly curled black hair (it does not occur to her that he is Jewish) and an ill-defined style characterised by a pale-blue parka she later discovers his sister bought for him as protection against the Oxford rain. A little shy, he chats to her about his New York background and casually throws out an invitation 'Why don't you come over and visit?' 'Actually, I've already been, thanks' Zoe replies, hard to impress. She is impressed though, in spite of herself, by his exceptional skill and relaxed confidence in academic debate, going to the heart of the Oxford arrogance. Is philosophy really the master-discipline? Why not literature? Doesn't literature also express profound truths about the world? She starts to pay attention. His irreverence is uplifting, oxygen in the miasmic atmosphere of Oxford academics.

It is the early 80s and the immensely positive energy of the American students, not intimidated by the insularity, atrophy and old-world cynicism that is the worst side of Oxford college life, is a breath of fresh air from a huge continent where everything seems possible, the place where the future is happening.

It is not until the reading party in Scotland in June, talking through long light midsummer evenings stretching out past midnight, that they start to get to know each other in the small eccentric group of students and a comfortable companionship evolves.

Paul goes back to the US for the summer.

Zoe becomes aware she is missing him, and he must be thinking about her as she receives a postcard from New York mainly about a social work case which has distressed him (no romance as yet). When he returns, he has ditched the parka and been up to Camden Lock and got his hair cut into a sharp black post-punk wedge and one ear pierced, with a tiny diamond chip in it. Apparently his father didn't like the standard-issue gold stud. 'Oooh! Who is this person?' They soon become inseparable, talking intently about all their visions for the future and decide to move into a graduate flat together. College regulations stipulate occupants should be married, so they get engaged.

Paul joins a band and plays the summer balls; Zoe discovers that he is a semi-professional drummer and singer and loves dancing. She is surprised by his insouciance on failing his Elizabethan handwriting exam; he points out that a lack of competence in deciphering 16th century manuscripts is unlikely to prevent him completing his PhD on the novels of Doris Lessing. He passes the resit and she notices that he looks rather nice in his white shirt and black academic gown.

Zoe starts a study group on French feminists and Paul has come to Oxford to do his PhD with a well-known left-wing professor. The next step seems almost certain to involve a move to the US. They discuss their future plans, and Zoe spends a whole day in tears at the thought of going to America, leaving family and friends behind. Yet she knows she has already 'swerved' from her own planned trajectory, as Michelle Obama so neatly puts it. She is in the process of adapting, following her instinct that she has found her life partner.

Looking back at those two young people, happy and light-hearted, framed for posterity in their engagement photo in a restaurant in New York, Zoe sees above all the fluidity of two young adults, still 'becoming' and malleable and open to whatever the future will be, trusting simply that they will work things out together.

Pisces

I am in my element
Body weightless
Held by the water
Bright blue sky sun trees
Outside it's winter
Here sunlight pours through the high glass wall

Lying back
I feel the strength in my shoulders
Arms slice the water legs kick
Breathe
Time is suspended
I am 8 years old 18 28
I follow the line of the beam on the ceiling
Slow down as I see the finish flags
Strung out above me
Toes find the ledge
I stand
Look across the pool to find you

I see your strong arms
Muscular smooth pale
Placing hands precisely on the skin of the water
Purposeful focused no splash
Turn and go again

Not Working!

Today I get up later after talking with Agnieszka into the small hours ... just like old student days but a bit stunned now I am 59 not 19. It doesn't matter. I am not working now! I go through the usual steadying morning routines, tea hits and I feel human again, my mind starts to clear. Agnieszka arrives to continue her PhD dissertation; we are both laughing, a bit dazed.

It is a beautiful mild blue sky day without a cloud, the little cherry tree with its sharp barely-there scent like old-fashioned sweets is in full bloom. Clumps of G's tiny daffodils are starring the ground underneath it, with heavy-scented white hyacinths and pink and blue feverfew sprinkled in between. A piece of her and a piece of spring is here, though it is not yet the end of February.

I must be outside today, no errands, not a day for tackling the desk. Quickly I wash and pull on old leggings a hoodie and my Convers. I must get out! Like Moley, I am muttering 'Hang spring cleaning!' and so happy with my plan. I scoff a beetroot and cheddar sandwich without sitting down, fill up my water bottle and clip it on my bike and stuff a protein bar in my paniers. It has been a long winter without taking my bike out and I have forgotten my routines. I decide the tyres are fine; I am too impatient to pump them up and jump on the bike. Like Toad, I am filled with the joy of bowling along the road, legs strongly pushing against pedals, gears clicking, I am off!

Dad gave me this love of cycling expeditions! I think and remember cycling this same route with the girls too. My skin feels the blissful warmth of the sun on my face and I am at the railway bridge. I sit in the sun on the old wooden mounting block, sheltered from the breeze by the old brick arches and the wall flanking the bridge, and take photos of the huge old trees standing solitary and still leafless in the centre of the iridescent emerald fields, so I can share this moment with everyone. A few cyclists pass by with conspiratorial smiles ... we know how lucky we are to be out in this glorious weather. I rest my eyes on the strong bare silhouette of the lone tree in the centre of the brilliant green field and it is a meditation without words.

Home ... can I get up the hill after so long inactive? I am conscious that here is now a van behind me which cannot pass on the narrow lane. I decide to speed up and surprisingly easily I am at the halfway point, a bend with a farm entrance where the van can easily pass me. I make a thumbs up sign to the driver to thank him for his patience and waves cheerfully out of his window. It is my day! I pedal steadily on, and to my astonishment I make it all the way to the brow of the hill, I see an elderly Asian couple smiling gently at me and I wave, quite triumphant that my body can still summon up this energy.

Agnieszka is in PhD-world, just leaving, and I make her jump moving silently in my Convers towards the house.

She laughs when I explain my ride and my book group meeting this evening. I make her stop an instant to smell the cherry blossom and see the daffodils and the sunlight on the garden. I am full of energy, oil and prick a baked potato, get out just-in-date fish and broccoli and then I am in the little conservatory, glass walls and roof extending the sun-filled day. Like Agnieszka I start some writing, slow to start but soon reluctant to let it go as I pick up the thread and ideas start to flow. Hunger stops me and I eat fast, I am loose-limbed after the cycling and set off early. For once I will be on time for book group!

The Sculpture Class

"I am going to tell you to stop worrying and just put the plaster on your form!" Alerted by the abruptness and fearing that I have exasperated her beyond bearing, I step back, look at the wire form I have made and realise I love it, despite the unexpectedly nerve-wracking struggle of the last two hours bending and stretching the honeycomb net to make my seashell. I have learned that the delicate wire structure has memory: once crushed it cannot spring back into the shape it had before. The spiral form is asymmetrical and lumpy, its surface dented where my inexperienced hands have applied too much pressure to it in my haste to complete the project, but there is something of the sea about it, rolled and pounded by the ocean.

I am sixty, but like a small child I am constantly seeking reassurance, vulnerable and anxious to hear that I am doing the right thing. With effort, she has restrained herself from intervening, despite her concern to ensure all her students create something that pleases them. There is a sense of the stubbornness in both of us, as I cling to my almost unattainable vision and she refuses to help me any further.

I wet the plaster strips and bandage my wire shell with the slippery white fabric. Sure enough it is transformed miraculously into a solid sculpture and I am lost in my absorption in the task. The next day, decorating my hollow seashell is a joy; I painstakingly line the wire inside with some soft oyster grey crinkled tissue paper, pressing on confidently and unhesitatingly as the lining reveals the cave-like quality of the shell's interior space. Inspired by a memory of glinting sea-water and sparkling sand, I sprinkle tiny foil discs of scintillating colours into the pool formed by the opening of the shell and illuminate the grotto from within with a tiny torch, marking its white exterior with faint pastel purple, brown and pink striations of iridescent powder. "I like that" says Barbara.

Kissing Frogs

Hands in her pockets and coat swinging loose she was striding down the wide street listening to some old favourite Motown tracks on her new headphones. She couldn't resist looking at herself in the shop windows as she passed. She was pleased with what she saw. Her bright green mac was so in at the moment, and she knew it looked good with her tall slim figure and smooth black skin and cropped hair. Even her green headphones matched her outfit. She felt confident, excited; spring was on its way and she was going to meet a new man. Ok, Rosanna, so you're not twenty any more, more like forty, she laughed to herself, but you can still look good when you want to. Should do this more often, girl.

However, as she got nearer to the rendez-vous, she began to feel nerves kicking in. That last guy she met, he had knocked her confidence, said she was 'interesting' but then made those odd comments ... sometimes you look stunning, and sometimes you look a bit rubbish ... When they kissed, there was a connection that surprised her, but that had led her astray in the past; she felt unsure of herself with him and unnerved by the sudden violent rows that blew up between them. When she asked why his relationship broke down, he could only say that he 'got bored'.

She thought of her own relationship with her husband; how her son had once asked her, 'Mum, if Dad were still alive now, do you think you would still be together ?' She had given the question some thought, and then said 'Yes'. They had had their ups and downs like everyone but it had been a good relationship. They had met at university, with no money but endless time. So much easier to get to know someone that way than on the internet, she mused, but all her friends had encouraged her, 'That's the way it is these days' , and she felt that her boys were old enough to understand; after all, they both had girlfriends themselves now. Now the joke was on her when she was late home: 'What kind of time is this to be coming in ?' they chorused gleefully on the rare occasions when they caught her creeping in. With her late shifts at the hospital, she got away with it most of the time.

She pushed nervously at the heavy plate glass door of the building, aware that perhaps her date might already be inside, watching her struggle awkwardly with the big scrolled handle, and then she heard a low chuckle behind her. An arm snaked past her, a big competent hand pushed the door open and she almost fell into the foyer. Turning to face each other, they both laughed. He was easy to recognise from the photo on the website; she liked his slightly loose jeans and his big hoodie, a bit more relaxed than the other guy, and his spontaneous grin. He had suggested meeting at the Museum of Modern Art to look at the new installations there. They chatted about the unusually sunny spring weather and exchanged some information about themselves, then fell into companionable silence, gasping from time to time at the extraordinary visions that met their eyes in each new room they walked into. Occasionally she stole a quick sideways glance at him, taking in his long face, the deep blue eyes and the freckles on his fair skin. From time to time she could feel his eyes on her too and she could tell he liked her.

From his profile she knew that he had three teenage children, of similar ages to her boys as it turned out. On the phone he had explained that he ran a research lab at the university and could sometimes get very absorbed in his experiments. Over lunch, he was careful to explain that he and his ex-wife were on good terms, they had just drifted apart when she started her own business and she had met someone else and left. The children had their own social lives now and everyone was quite flexible about arrangements. He's taking me seriously, she registered. He had kept the big family house and the children came and went on sleep-overs and holidays with friends, much like her own boys. With his highly specialised academic work, he was unlikely to move from the department. She had clung to her family and career for survival when Richard died and she knew she did not want to leave her lifelong friends and long-established roots in the city. 'You have to kiss a lot of frogs,' her friend had said. She felt something inside her decide, 'Ok, I think I'm going to give this one a go.'

Race Against Time

Once again I need to get to the station a little faster than humanly possible in the time available. Setting off at a brisk run, to my chagrin I am forced to reduce my pace to a very fast walk as I am now a little older and a little heavier and find myself somewhat out of breath on the uphill slopes. I repeat this process 5 or 10 times, saving vital minutes by taking a short cut through to the main road and crossing it on a long diagonal while the lights are on red and the traffic on hold. Practising my calming yoga breathing I arrive at the precipitous flight of crumbling concrete steps down to the station, where I make myself slow down and place my feet carefully on the too shallow slippery little ledges, remembering how much damage it is possible to do falling onto a hard surface and the X-ray photo of my titanium-pinned complex compound left wrist fracture.

From the top deck of the bus waiting at the traffic lights, Hugh observes this phenomenon and as I turn up, windswept but very proud of my sprint, just in time for our train, I am greatly amused and somehow gratified to be informed that this routine, first evolved as a child running to the school bus stop in the mornings, not only has a name, 'interval training', but also is how top athletes build up fitness. I make him laugh relating how astonished my daughter was in Palermo to see me suddenly take off and run for the train to the seaside, determined not to miss our day out at the beach. There is something just so liberating and joyful about a burst of speed, feeling the strength of your legs propelling your body like a freely running horse. Setting off in plenty of time is just not the same.

On the Water

Zoe had signed up for this trip a couple of months ago, attracted by the idea of being on the water in a narrowboat on a summer afternoon. So many pleasant associations ... Ratty and Moley messing about in boats ... the countryside in summer ... memories of floating gently along in her friend's boat, chatting and munching sandwiches. And there was that away day she had managed to organise aboard Colin's old narrowboat, watching him expertly manoeuvring the long vehicle past the other boats, patiently shouting instructions as they ran up and down the steps to the lock gates and swung the barge into the lock pool, often only inches wider than the boat. Zoe remembered the calm green confluence of waterways, populated nowadays only by leisure boats and a few live-in narrowboats.

Still, literary and fanciful as she was, she was not in danger of idealising the boatmen's lives. She remembered her friend's tales of growing up on a working boat, one of the last people to remember transporting goods around the country on the canals as their families had done for generations. Seldom spending long enough in one place for her to go to school, Susan grew up unable to read. There might be ten or twelve children in a family. Susan would steer the boat as a child while her parents were busy with other work or children. A premature baby was put in bowl of warm olive oil to keep it alive and fed with a pipette. As her way of life came to an end with the advent of motorways and road haulage companies transporting goods by lorry, Susan, ever feisty and resourceful, became a foundry supervisor.

A boat full of older women ... Zoe was a bit unnerved. She felt too young for this. She realised she had spent most of her life with men. Her childhood memories were all of adventures with her brother, climbing trees, riding bikes, making a table in the garage with her father, until, miraculously, a girl of her own age moved into her street. During her student days in Oxford, male students outnumbered females five to one in the university. Many of her good friends from those days, who had remained close, were men. And then, working at the Technical College, with engineers, electricians, chemists ... She was not used to group outings either, she realised, and perhaps she had been thinking more of *Three Men in a Boat* rather than 28 women in a narrowboat.

Zoe picked out the faces she recognised and made an effort to recall names. Clare was there, with her soft voice and gentle, considerate manner, and there was Jane, quiet but with a sly sense of humour, a little shy, perhaps. And Louise, who organised the Book Group, and always looked out for her. Zoe chatted to Clare, who listened patiently, ever the social worker, to her concerns about her daughter's boyfriend and she and Jane discussed the closure of the library and the effects of Government cuts on children's services in the city. Zoe felt pleased to be a member of this eclectic and companiable group of women. The trip was giving everyone such pleasure, an eagerly-awaited opportunity to get out for some fun and laughter.

Most of the group had no interest in going out on the tiny deck area at the front of the boat. Louise beckoned to her to come out and sit with her and Zoe squeezed herself onto the little bench, relishing the cool fresh air after long hot dry summer, the slow movement of the water past the sides of the boat, travelling at walking pace, talking in a desultory fashion about whatever came into their heads. Again Zoe picked up the unease at the huge changes in the city: the University buying up all the old houses; the brash new tower blocks of student accommodation; the massive inflation of house prices; the developers ignoring the desperate need for social housing which Zoe had become so aware of in her work with the migrants and refugees. The city was only just coping.

The boat slid past the modern flats right on the waterside, a recent initiative which aroused her curiosity. Zoe imagined it all bustling with cafes and city living families. Under the overhanging branches of the damson trees, she spotted a moorhen with two tiny black chicks, obviously unafraid of the passers-by. A cyclist passed by on the towpath. The slow pace of the canals, but within the city limits. Dreamily she murmured to herself, perhaps this is the answer.

Part 10
Educating Myself

A Time to Speak

A time to grieve a time to heal
A time to speak a time to be still
A time to rejoice a time to console
A time to listen and a time to leave

A time to rest a time to dance
A time to plant a time to clear away
A time to cry a time to sing out
A time to hold close and a time to let go

* For AH

Educating Myself

My grandfather was a Labour MP and perhaps I had inherited his 'bolshiness.' Of course, we were not revolutionaries, merely subversive elements in a girls' direct grant school which had changed little in its ethos since the 1950s. As we reached the Sixth Form we made it our business to undermine the authority of the old guard of teachers, with the tacit support of many of the more progressive element.

Determined to break the mould, we created a plethora of student roles on the committee of our school magazine to outnumber the staff involved and produced the first ever magazine entirely edited by the girls. At morning assembly, we played John Lennon, watching the headmistress's expression morph from relief at the beautiful melody to horror at the words

Imagine there's no countries
It isn't hard to do
Nothing to kill or die for
And no religion too ...

After a blameless school career, I finally crossed the line in the last year, when I was told I could not wear small gold studs in my newly-pierced ears while the holes healed. Our school was in the centre of the county town, and old ladies reported us for going out at lunchtime without wearing our hats. (We voted to get rid of them too eventually). I was not allowed into classes, so I did my 'A' Level revision in the school library, which probably suited me better. My parents, both lecturers, were supportive. After all, this was the punk era, and, living in Coventry, I was used to seeing boys and girls my age clad in studded black leather, hair in blue or red Mohican crests like exotic birds, with elaborate tattoos and silver chains from nose to ear.

On our last day, a life-size stuffed doll dressed in our very distinctive uniform appeared at the window of the Sixth Form block, suspended by its school tie. I heard later that soon after our departure our headmistress left and became a Buddhist nun.

I see myself at Oxford, younger than most because I would not stay an extra year at school and outnumbered 5:1 by men. With little social mix, my African-Caribbean friend left after a few weeks; I very nearly did the same. The 8-week terms were so intense that working in a café in the vacations felt like a relief at times. The grandson of Sainsbury was awarded a place at one college just as the family donated a new library. A huge banner appeared the next day across the façade: *Good colleges cost less at Sainsbury's.*[*] I felt I had a duty to stay, otherwise nothing would ever change; when I eventually found my feet, I made friendships there that were to last for the rest of my life.

---

[*] the slogan at the time was *Good food costs less at Sainsbury's*

And slowly Oxford worked its magic. Living in such a beautiful place, wandering down lanes not changed in hundreds of years, between the high stone walls of colleges and gardens dating back to the Middle Ages, I slipped back in time. Where else would I have found myself in a book-lined study at the top of a 16th-century tower, discussing the development of the French language in the 5th-8th centuries over a glass of madeira with a tutor who spoke at least 7 languages? There were legendary deluges of rain, cold wet dark days when I was glad to take refuge in the library. There were hot summer days punting sleepily along the backwaters, maybe skinny-dipping from the boat after a few glasses of wine. And formal dinners in ancient halls where I was offered snuff after dessert and wobbled unsteadily home on my bike.

From there to the freedom of my teaching assistant post in equally historic and much sunnier Montpellier on my year abroad in France. Reluctant to return, I did not fit back into college well and was admonished by the Dean for not doing enough work; it was my final year. I did not know where I fitted in at all, but made it into postgraduate work and had a few more precious years to find out.

Mine was an indirect route into teaching in Further Education. Like most people, I had never understood what it was, despite the fact my father was a lecturer at the Technical College for twenty years.

Teaching adults …*The University of the Second Chance* … I loved it and never looked back.

Home Visit

In the labyrinth of the council estate
I find your house
Basic but clean and neat
You are attractive youthful dark-haired Westernised
A professional woman hoping to pick up her career
Your teenage son brings me coffee and water
I have guessed right and he is delighted with the
Winter jacket I chose for him
Your little girl is affectionate and sits up close beside me
Your middle child I know has some unspecified
    learning difficulty
She is restless and paces around the strange new
    environment
I bring warm coats for all of you
Blankets duvets pillows
Curtains for your windows
Pans mugs kitchen implements
You already have some from the local church you have
Started attending
We talk and you explain
My husband was killed by Isis
He had become a Catholic and
We all converted with him
They took him out and shot him

The first house they found us was
On the other side of the city

We could not stay there
The streets were full of men who looked to us
Just like the ones who killed him
We brighten up the living room
With turquoise silky cushions
A rug and some new curtains
I am a widow too I say
It's all that I can offer but maybe
Better than nothing
And I will bring some winter shoes

Choose Hope

If you behave aggressively towards our staff, we will have you removed from the plane.

Zoe could not believe her ears. She was one of the last to reach her seat after an exhausting transit from the boarding gate, standing for half an hour in a long crowded claustrophobic tunnel with no emergency exit, and was longing to sit down. A flight attendant appeared and told her she was going to removing her bag and put it in the hold. Zoe explained that she was travelling with her daughter and needed to keep her bag with her to make a connection in London.

I think you are lying.

The flight attendant pointed to some illegible biro scrawl on the baggage sticker and accused her of trying to sneak the bag on despite the coding. Zoe had never travelled with carry-on luggage before. She had no idea what this woman was talking about.

The situation suddenly seemed to spin into a nightmare scenario as Zoe found herself threatened by the senior cabin crew with being taken off the flight. Zoe took a deep breath and explained that she was annoyed because she had just had been accused of lying. How could anyone describe her behaviour as aggressive ?

She began to wonder if she had her old University staff ID card on her or any other evidence of good character. How could you prove you were a 'normal' person ? She pointed to the space in the rack above her head and explained again that she was travelling with her daughter and needed to make a connection. As suddenly as it had begun, the confrontation was over; the offending tag was removed, the bag placed in the rack and Zoe took her seat.

There was a sympathetic grimace from the man in the aisle seat and Zoe's daughter was just a few rows away, but if things had gone against me, would anyone have stood up for me ? Zoe wondered. It was the word of the attendant against mine. No-one had supported her. Everyone had kept their heads down. For the first time in her whole life, she was experiencing how it felt to be confronted with someone in uniform who had the power to decide that you were not going to return home, even though you had done nothing wrong. The confrontation and the rush of adrenalin had left her feeling agitated and shaky.

She thought of the refugee whose ten-year-old daughter had been removed from a plane and was still in another country, thousands of miles away, months later, awaiting a stamp on her visa to rejoin her mother. Ela had told her of the dispute she had had over the DNA test requested by the Home Office for her child, which she had had to save up for months to pay for. Detained and publicly humiliated, having to provide evidence for random checks, always under suspicion, how often this was experience of the asylum seekers she worked with.

There were some who could not withstand that constant uncertainty and anxiety. Richard told her that counsellors were now placing asylum seekers on suicide watch.

Only a few days later, a sixty-nine-year-old East Asian doctor on an American airline was randomly asked to leave the plane because the flight was over-booked. Like Zoe, he had remonstrated with the flight attendant, as he had patients to attend to at his destination. Mobile phone video from other horrified passengers showed him being pushed to the floor, lip split open and face bleeding, and dragged off the plane by his ankles. The video went viral on Facebook; boycotts were organised; the airline director was fired. For once Zoe rejoiced in the power of social media. She thought of another image which had caught everyone's imagination, a peaceful one, a young Asian woman smiling at a snarling EDL demonstrator in Birmingham, protecting a young woman in a headscarf from his abuse. Hope not Hate read the banners.

Hope is the mechanism whereby human beings heal themselves and restore their equilibrium.

A Place of Safety

For George Floyd*

The burly man on the video
Has a light stubble
Slightly defensive
Slightly apologetic
He shows the discreet gate in the wire mesh
Hospital security fencing
Carefully signposted
'Place of Safety'
This is where the police bring you in
When they section you
We do our best to be welcoming
First impressions are very important
The corridor is clean modern newly decorated
The interview room small but has
Brand new comfortable padded blue armchairs
Wipe clean everything
It is a bit bare he concedes
But we have to always be mindful of safety
At the reception
Bags are searched and sharps removed

---

* Written a year before the death of George Floyd after viewing a
video about mental health services

Another Planet

You say it doesn't matter
Which words I use
Coloured foreigner
Everyone knows I'm not a racist
This pc language thing has become
Ridiculous

I say people who don't know you
Only hear
The words you say
If you use the same words as racists
How do they know you are
Not one too?

We choose to use this pc language for a reason
To stand with anyone who finds herself abused
And to say clearly to everyone
You and all your community are welcome here

And if you heard a young man shout
You in there you'll soon be leaving
Outside the corner shop on the high street

And if you saw an old woman spat at
On the bus home in central London
Notwithstanding her British passport

And if your child was told at school by the other
    children
You'll be going 'home' now

Would you still say that the words we use
Don't matter ?

What planet do you live on?

Keeping Faith

We are on stage now, in St Michael's Guildhall, the great mediaeval stone and glass tracery behind us and the audience of the Lord Mayor and assorted dignitaries and guests in front. In our motley 'wear what you like as long as it's red and black' choir outfits, I reflect that we must be quite a contrast to the general run of performers here. I am proud of the Mayor and the city for inviting us to perform, proud of the banner of Youth and Diversity which won Coventry the bid for the City of Culture 2021, proud of my Worldsong choir, proud of our exuberant musical director Una May Olomolaiye MD. We are singing a song from Kenya for Yasmin Alibhai-Brown, though at the moment she is invisible in the crowded room. Soon Una May has everyone up singing and dancing with us and even the most cynical cannot resist. *Keeping Faith in Just Values in an Age of Populism* ... the title of the talk and the speaker appealed to me and it is why I am singing here tonight, but the power of voice and rhythm by-passes the intellectual wording and goes straight to the heart of the message. *Freedom is coming, Oh yes, I know.*

Yasmin describes herself as 'a leftie liberal, anti-racist, feminist, Muslim, part-Pakistani.' She is a well-known and often controversial journalist, author and academic writing on immigration, diversity and multiculturalism issues. In contrast to some of the powerful and hard-hitting articles by her that I remember reading, Yasmin is a tiny, birdlike figure with bright eyes and sharp features, speaking slowly and gently. She sets the scene with two incidents, one when she was a young woman on a London bus in the 70s and someone spat at her and called her a Paki. We are saddened but not surprised. That was what happened then. The other is the same incident, but it happened this year, to this woman now almost 70 who has been here now for almost 50 years. And she proceeds to examine why. In the wake of Brexit anti-immigrant campaigning, after the referendum some people believed all immigrants would have to leave. I am so impressed by her erudition and insight that I resolve to buy her latest book *Exotic England* and find out about the history of diversity in my own country, which I realise I am shamefully ignorant of.

Yasmin walks us through the policies and initiatives of multiculturalism and its limitations to the place she has reached, where we will still respect each other, but we will each question and explore honestly the other's culture and its norms. I enjoy her facility with conceptualising the latest thinking, dynamic interculturalism. 'For example', she says, 'I cannot respect the binge-drinking culture of the UK'. I am reminded of my university classroom with my international graduate students, Muslim and non-Muslim, from every country and culture, hammering out their views on this very topic and many others. I hope that somewhere in the world they are continuing the discussion and I am glad when Yasmin says that young people are her reason for hope. With engaging modesty, she does not stop there, and talks entertainingly and humbly about her own blind spot, her difficulty with grasping the issues around transsexuals, and how her daughter had to give her a one-hour lecture to bring her up to date. A breath of fresh air. Thank you, Yasmin.

The minder is at the back of the hall, just behind my seat, and I see that he is chafing and impatient to remove his charge to the safety of the warm train back to London. There is a moment when Yasmin is standing right beside me, looking absent-mindedly for her coat in true academic fashion and a little reluctant to leave, and I have a childish desire to say something, then the small figure disappears into the November night.

Entertaining Angels

For Nawal, Bahraa and Maysaa
Sept 2017*

I look up and they are here. Three still, bright, radiant figures, flames of turquoise, peach and sapphire, heads swathed in fine silk scarves.

The space is filled with the loud excited exchanges of the regular migrant women, squabbling and sociable, like black and white magpies, grabbing clothing, nappies, food to last the week.

Still, strong and dignified, the three stand straight and calm in the crowded waiting room.

The week before, I knock at their homes, noticing the Arabic blessing over the door, a carefully casual visitor in my jeans. They are welcoming but sombre figures, in their worn black home clothes, bringing me bitter black coffee and sweet cakes. This morning, I am the shabby one, offering tea and toast and jam.

Outside, two young-ish men, excluded from the women's centre, are waiting. One is slim and silent, standing patiently; the other, his face smiling and animated, his body twisted and without movement in an electric wheelchair. The husbands.

With the interpreter, we sit together and we talk. We piece together the jigsaw of English and Arabic, work out how to help .

They have not come for food or clothing, bedding or knives and forks. They have come for orthopaedic mattresses, wheelchairs and laptops.

Humbled by their trust, I wonder, what were their lives before ? Syria is not much in the news these days.

---

* I wrote this after a morning at the centre for refugees, asylum seekers and migrants run by Carriers of Hope in Coventry. The title comes from the Bible verse: 'Do not neglect to show hospitality to strangers, for thereby some have entertained angels unawares.' (Hebrews 13:2)

An Ibo Person

I have met a quiet person
Who tells me he is from Eastern Nigeria
An Ibo person
I guessed it but I was not sure
I remember the novel we read at book group
Half of a Yellow Sun
The story of Biafra
Which I can only dimly recall
I was a child of eight and
It was all over when I was eleven
I looked up the history
The bid for freedom
The brutal response*
My mother hid from me
The starving children
The terrible photos
Too late released to the world
The Ibo were democratic
With no chiefs or rulers
That did not suit the British

Well my quiet Ibo person
Listens while I tell of my
Weekend in Paris my night at the opera
He tells me he likes Eurostar
Better than flying
I think of all he has been through

Studying Shakespeare at his Anglican grammar school
PhD promising career but never returned
He lost a wife and a child
A country a future
I am humbled and once more reminded
Of how easily we take all that we have
For granted

Part 11

Theatre

350 Years of the Opera Garnier

Under the stage of the Opera Garnier in Paris, there is a subterranean lake hundreds of yards across. Who knows? Perhaps this is the secret space that gave rise to the myth of the Phantom of the Opera. Anything seems possible here. So graceful from afar, an iconic building like a colonnaded wedding cake, paeon to an Emperor, tympanum surmounted by a neo-classical turquoise dome and implausibly huge, angel-like figures covered in gold, gleaming in the sunlight as if they have just alighted. We make out the name of one ... Harmony.

As we approach, we see that each of the sea-green lamp-posts is supported by a goddess and bears a small plaque, 'Restored thanks to the generosity of ...' For a moment, I imagine myself philanthropically sponsoring a lamp-post ... somehow it does not seem unreasonable in front of this wildly extravagant and slightly delusional palace of the arts. Up, up the massive stone steps we go, past the groups of students and the tour guides, but how to get in ? To one side, dwarfed by the portico, a surreal empty metal door frame we must walk through is the only intrusion of twenty-first century security; of course, we have not long ago seen *Un Ballo in Maschera*, based on the assassination of Gustave III of Sweden, fatally wounded and borne through the crowds on a bier from the opera house he built.

We enter, awed by the immense hall, entranced by the statues, the staircases, the gilded and painted ceilings. We are hundreds of spectators, but this space is brightly-lit and somehow also intimate, as if we are guests of Napoleon or Eugenie. Laughing and pointing, we photograph everything. From above, we capture our fellow-guests drifting up the double flight of steps and passing under four great golden harmonious circles suspended from the roof. It is a few moments before our eyes understand that we are looking at tractor tyres covered in gently glowing gold leaf.

Up, up to the next floor and the usher who chats as we wind through the arcane passageways to the opera boxes. 'It is not just beautiful, it is unique in the whole world' he proclaims proudly, entirely justified as nothing in our experience can hold a candle to this place. Like cognoscenti, we exchange opera gossip with him: the extraordinary performance we went to at the Bastille the night before, where the exquisite soprano injured her foot and the second half had to be cancelled. She is ok, he informs us, it was just her toe. In compensation, we have been offered tickets to another performance and we are already planning our return.

Our box is a delightful small room, papered in soft red damask; there are simple elegant dark wooden chairs with red velvet-cushions and a red velvet canape to recline upon should we feel weary. We imagine our friends next door, visiting in the interval for champagne and oysters. We gaze at the opulent interior of the theatre and realise that we are behind a mirror-image of the glorious façade of the gilded balconies opposite us across the auditorium. Elaborate initials E and N designate the seats reserved for the Emperor and his wife in the front circle. I look up at the brilliantly-coloured dancers and creatures on the ceiling, painted more recently by Chagall around a dazzling chandelier the size of a small meteorite, lean out as far as the vertiginous drop below will allow me and snap and send a Whatsapp home.

So close to the stage that we feel the music vibrating through us, we know now we have fallen under the irresistible, delusional spell of Garnier's fabulous opera house, which can never be undone.

Contralto Profondo

Last week I sang the bass part at choir
It did not go down very low
And I could manage it easily
Anne and I stood with the men
(The woman bass was singing tenor)
I felt the deep pulse of the voices
How it felt to be a very low lady
Contralto profondo
Slightly transgressive
Fun and surprising
Just for one song

Cirque du Soleil

Up on the high wire again
Exhilarating
Don't look down

Katrina at the Ballet

Thick sparkling silver hair falling heavy to her
   shoulders
Diva calmly sitting in her soft purple evening dress
Plunging neckline graceful light folds tumbling to her feet
It's her red carpet night Katrina at the ballet
I hope when I am in my eighties I will be just like her ...
I lean over and ask her friend How much can she see
   and hear?
We think she sees a whirl of colour bursts of movement
   maybe patterns
She will hear the music's rhythms and feel the bass
   vibrating
The strumming of the drums the thrum of dancers' feet
   in time so close to us
Many years now she's been hard of hearing isolated
I go to talk to her Hello Katrina it's Fiona
She pulls me in and hugs me tight says
I'm having such a wonderful time
Love being out with all of you
In the group being sociable
You see when I began to lose my sight my husband
   rejected me
Determined beautiful joyful strong she
Clasps me firmly speaks into my hair
I'm lost for words instead I sense
Her gift to me
Humility

Transgressive

I like the notion of transgressive behaviours
Gender as performative
Not given at birth
Just one thing
Fluidity and choice
Breaking the mould
A bride for the *Bartered Bride*
A whole BAME orchestra

I hear on the radio
Trump Putin Boris Johnson
Toxic and disturbing
Traditional unreconstructed masculinity
I'm waiting for the day
The next generation
When just like smoking
No-one remembers
How it *used to be*

---

[*] 'There are some very disturbing models of a traditional toxic type
of masculinity in roles of power at the moment' Radio 4 interview

Yuli

A girl walks on the wave-drenched harbour wall, Havana, unseeing in her madness. Opening her arms, she falls into the stormy bosom of the ocean, finds her peace. It is your sister.

A boy leaps blindly on the London stage, lonely, dreaming of home. Twisting his foot, he falls into the deep oblivion of pain. It's you, Carlos Acosta.

Will you dance again ?

It is a way out, back to Cuba, you stay there, with family, with friends. Your father shuns you. Violence cracks the air. You made those dances from the beatings that he gave you, when you ran away from school. And you must dance that story, pain and loneliness, there's no way back to your old world.

So you're world famous, but you don't forget your dream, to resurrect the revolutionary National School of Dance for everyone, lost in the ravine. Not just a dancer, you're an artist. First black Romeo, forbidden love, we welcome you and in return, you remake us our ballet, bring us a Don Quixote full of joy, the gypsies individual and bold, crowd chatting on the stage,

---

* *Yuli* is a film about the Cuban ballet dancer Carlos Acosta

puppet horse life-size trotting through the squares of hot sun-drenched Havana. Thank you.

Soaked to the skin by the storm outside, we watch the film, my daughter and I, crying, laughing, shocked, delighted, grieving with you and rejoicing.

I am a mother and a father too. I know we all give beatings, push our children out into the world, no way back home, each to make their own story.

Non-binary

The signs say 'changing village'
'Gender neutral changing room'
There is a 'male' changing room
It seems I've ended up in there
Somehow I lost my partner
But all is well
I put my things in a locker
Choose a cubicle and
Start to get out my bikini
Meanwhile a pleasant young man
Opens the door
Which I have not yet locked
And laughs to find
A woman in there
It is a Midsummer Night's Dream
And we are all mechanics lovers fairies
I love the confusion
Children wander through the forest
I stay in the 'male' cubicle
Can't be bothered to move my stuff
Later I find a hidden pathway
That takes me to the 'female' ones
We are in Shakespeare's country
In the ancient Forest of Arden[*]
A non-binary world no clumsy labels LGBITQA
And long may it continue

---

[*] In Shakespeare's day all parts were played by men, with boys in the women's roles

Part 12

Remembering

Charleston

We are jigging up and down flapping our elbows to the old-time music, laughing and out of breath. It is the Charleston and neither of us can do it. It is not the music of your youth, but your mother's, my grandmother, Evelyne, who was by all accounts a very good dancer and told me that when she was young she once put a five pound note in her shoe to go out and wore it to shreds in one night on the dance floor.

It is a joy to see you prancing about and laughing because you always had such a sharp sense of humour and loved play-acting and now that is seldom there. It seems people with Alzheimer's rarely laugh, but you are responding to the familiar music, a collection of 1920s and 30s songs on a favourite CD from Upton Hall, and I am sure it is taking you back to days with your mother, in another century. We are waving our hands around and strutting around the small room having fun and then just as you are getting tired, there is a knock at the door and a carer comes in with the afternoon cup of tea and biscuits. We listen to the rest of the tracks and before long we are both asleep in the soft armchairs, in a gentle companionable afternoon nap. Already I know that these are moments to treasure.

Narcissi

I bought these tiny yellow daffodils
Bulbs crammed into tiny pot
Because you loved them and
To help you know that outside
It is spring.
Later some white hyacinths
Spiky with sweet heavy scent
Because you always had them on your windowsill at
    home
To help you mark
The end of winter.
And when the flowers were gone
I saved the bulbs
I put them in my garden
Underneath the little cherry tree
And forgot
Year after year now
I look out
And you are gone
I miss you
But your flowers greet me
Every spring
And speak of hope

---

* My mother was in care with Alzheimer's for the last three years of her life

Theresa

I hardly know you
I have only just joined the choir
My neighbour introduced me to it
Came along for a few evenings
Til I was settled in
She didn't tell me it was a capella
With songs in at least ten different languages
And a concert at Christmas
I'd never sung in a choir before
You sing right beside me
I hear your strong voice in my ear
Pitch perfect
Body beside me moving with those
Challenging beautiful African rhythms
Listening always listening
You teach me how to learn by ear how to hear the
    others
And tell me
When I try to hide my voice in the crowd
She can hear you
She hears everyone
I'll give it a year I thought
Try not to give up

I didn't know how sick you were
Until the treatments started
Until your face changed

And the racking coughing sometimes stopped you
    singing
But only for a moment
I thought
I hardly know you
And now we are going to lose you
Just like I lost my husband
All those years ago
No way of knowing how long it will be
We sing together
They gave you a year I think
And you will not give up
Sing at the concert
Sing all through the summer
Singing and dancing with us
Until the day you died

The Stranger

I knew he was dead as soon as I saw him. His eyes were rolled right back up into his head and his skin was puffy and grey. His body was lying in a crumpled, untidy heap on the tarmac of his drive, not far from his car. He was not young, perhaps about 60, overweight and looked as if his clothes didn't quite fit, as if he had been stuffed into them like the Guys we used to make for Bonfire Night when we were little.

'Doctor Alison' knelt down and examined his neck for a pulse. Within seconds, she was shaking her head and gently pronouncing that there was nothing we could do for him. We felt a strange sense of calm and relief. Alison certified the death herself. There would be no cardio-pulmonary resuscitation, no violent attempts to rekindle life in this tired, old, worn-out body.

Marie was standing barefoot in the doorway across the road, silhouetted against the lighted foyer of the church hall, shouting to us ... Did we need a phone ? I realised she still didn't know the man we had found was dead. I walked back and told her and the other yoga student still waiting with her.

There was sadness for the man, this stranger we had found as we walked out of our yoga class, chatting and laughing, wishing each other a Happy Christmas and calling to each other 'See you in the New Year !' Sadness for his daughter, whom the police had contacted. Sadness for his little dog, stood shivering in the drive, waiting for him to open the front door and let it in.

And yet I felt that this was a good way to go. A sudden, quick fall, tumble into unconsciousness and eternity. There was a sense of heightened reality, intense awareness of our own energy and life force, how precious our time is.

It was too soon to go home. We left Alison to complete the procedures and packed Marie's equipment into her car, surprised at how much stuff she brings to every class for us, chatting quietly and reassuring ourselves with the normality of rolling up yoga mats, folding blankets, stowing her reading glasses carefully in the front with the music player to be sure she would find them when she got home.

The adrenalin rush we had all felt as we ran to the supine figure was subsiding as we stood and talked to the police and paramedics. There was no sign of foul play. The neighbours informed the police that he lived alone. The loose-limbed body was laid on the ambulance stretcher and more procedures were discussed. I felt detached. And then an arm fell out as they lifted him and a young paramedic quickly strapped it to the side, with a nervous laugh.

For a split second I connect with something buried deep in my own memory. I see again the ambulance paramedics gently strapping Paul into the chair to carry him downstairs, the last time he left the house. It was a very unusual large 60's spiral staircase, which I had slipped on more than once. Looking up from below, I noticed the gentle care of the paramedics, that same gesture securing the limbs before the strong arms lifted the chair and brought him down to the ambulance.

Someone has died. I turn away. It is time to go home.

The Shark

There is a shark swimming in a glass tank
Except that it is not moving, just hanging in the water
A prodigious feat of taxidermy
A corpse perfectly preserved
The title is
*The Physical Impossibility of Death in the Mind of
    Someone Living*
We had a sort of wake while Paul was still aware
And the consultant very delicately mentioned signing
    the will
The mind cannot imagine someone really gone, she said
There's not much time.

Time makes no sense at all I thought.
My godson, only four, asked every day
Paul's dead, isn't he?
But still the mind could not
Absorb that information.
One daughter first day back at school was sick
The last time she was there
Dad was alive
One brought home a photo of us all on holiday
Left up in a classroom display about *Families*
And even after many years I could wake up some days
    thinking
I must tell Paul ...

Farewell 2005

Grandad[*] in hospital no hearing aids no glasses thick dust under bed stained floor no pyjamas make consultant explain what is happening to him lights are going out all over brain mostly darkness now it is enough.

Move him to care home, peaceful garden view, carer apologises your father can't come off the drugs now, but he is dignified, hears us can see us, in his nice green M and S pyjamas, can say a few words, I point to the garden sounds like 'nice'. For those last few weeks there is care and respect.

In the chapel of rest I come to visit him, gather my thoughts, know he is gone. Just as he always was, face calm and handsome old man, old brown walking shoes, favourite green trousers and warm checked flannel shirt. One thing is not the same, it takes me a while to work it out, the undertakers have removed his small neat salt and pepper moustache. For the first time in my life in death I see him without it.

---

[*] My children named my parents G and Grandad and it stuck

Farewell 2015

I know to come this evening. Exhausted, first visit in a few days but now I feel sure it must be tonight. The ward is quiet and I am alone here, quiet in the little room and grateful for the privacy. G has not spoken or moved in days, face filled out and looking strangely younger eyes half shut unseeing or at least uncomprehending heavy coma-like body in bed.

I sit and listen to the sound of her breathing, regular calm not effortful just very long sibilant breaths from deep in the lungs I touch my mother's swollen arms look at her corpse-like form and know that it cannot be long. The woman priest has offered to come but I don't feel that's needed now.

I remember something I read recently, approach the bed and stroke her head, something I never did before, smoothing the short soft fine hair. The gesture is instinctive and the touch feels like words. I start to say softly, 'We are ok, you can go now.' Over and over gently repeat the words and then I leave.

At midnight I am woken by the call .

---

* Maya Angelou describing her farewell to her mother

The Gardener

Sometimes as I am gazing at the huge tree-shaded
   border
Taking in tall purple irises now coming into flower
Half-hidden behind the variegated shrub whose name I
   can't remember
Noticing something like cow parsley with deep red
   stems instead of green
New-planted little shrubs growing up graceful against
   the fence
Eye resting on the tranquil powder-blue-mauve
   ceanothus
As I am guessing where the picnic table and the seats
   will be
Creator of all this a little fey you silently appear beside
   me
And I laugh and say *Zilfa I conjured you up!*
Imagining the seat and table that we spoke of yesterday
I can see my mother sitting there newspaper open
Watching the red setters race across the *'little park'*
This is her gift and on the plaque we will just write
Enjoy

Acknowledgements

Thanks to all my friends, some of whom appear in the book, who took an interest and gave me such kind reviews.

In particular, I would like to thank the following people:

Jessica Eastman and the members of the creative writing group at the Coventry Resource Centre for the Blind for many stimulating hours at the classes and so much laughter

Jessica again for patiently editing my first very messy draft

Linda and all the members of my book group for such an encouraging and positive response to my first efforts at writing

Anne Harrison and Corinne Pithion for being my critical friends

My daughter Lucy for creative advice on the cover design

My daughter Chloe for her very perceptive comments on the text

Becky, Rebecca, Maire, Tasmin and all the team at Grosvenor House Publishing, who received the manuscript in its raw state and helped me to create a published book

Laura Nyahuye of Maokwo for her inspirational spoken word performances

Una May Olomolaiye for helping me to find my singing voice

About the author

Born near Newcastle, Fiona Kaplan studied languages at St Catherine's College, Oxford and taught mature students in Further and Higher Education. She divides her time between her family and friends, volunteering, theatre and travel and has recently started to experiment with writing and singing in a choir.

Lucy Swimming is her first collection of poems.

Lightning Source UK Ltd.
Milton Keynes UK
UKHW041204301120
374347UK00002B/47